VISION

Stephen Bello

The Sword of Excellence Publishing House

Published by
SWORD OF EXCELLENCE PUBLISHING HOUSE
For more information email
stephen2bello@yahoo.co.uk
or phone
+441634920491

'My people are destroyed for lack of knowledge(vision): because thou have rejected knowledge, I will also reject thee, but thou has forgotten the law of God, I will also forget thy   children.'

                                                                        HOSEA 4:6

PREFACE

Vision and wisdom are two of a kind, they are essentials we dare not do without in our daily lives if we want to fulfil the purpose for which we were created by all wise God as part of the world in our generation. The correct use or application of information we have access to is wisdom in its true essence. On the other hand, vision is the foresight, insight, and forward planning to apply wisdom gained effectively to bring optimum output or results for every investment made.

Vision therefore is indispensable for anyone who wants to be a highflyer or a consistent achiever in any field of endeavour. This quality will bring into your life the necessary determined disciplines needed to pull off successfully any plan or project you have at hand. The vision you have will drive you and make you commit to diligence and excellence in all you do in life. The spin off rewards of your diligence will be that you will stand out from the crowd of 'all others' in a unique club of the excellent.

In addition to these benefits, vision would build your character as a person to make you resilient in the face of difficulties that might come your way. The vision you have will keep you going again and again even if you must go after your dream goals seven times. Vision would develop in you a tenacity that in turn would make you a rare breed of person who will thrive in any situation never giving up on the objective that has been set before you. The inspired words of the holy scriptures and the various characters who showed the importance of the vision they had as it guided then provide a template that we all can follow to achieve the same greatness and outstanding results just like they did.

This book has been written out of a desire to see the many opportunities to both obtain and grow a God-given vision for our lives from the pages of scriptures as unfolded by the Holy Spirit. The insights gained are deep and yet practical in application to everyday life situations. Our saviour Jesus Christ invites us to come to Him as a sheep comes to the shepherd to obtain insight into the importance of a divine vision as we battle the challenges of daily shining in a very dark and depraved generation that seems to be moving further away from God year on year.

As ever, get ready to be challenged in your theology and understanding of scriptural perspectives as the Holy Spirit outlines peculiar insights that will in turn make you stand out from the crowd all the while learning at His feet. The greatest help you can give yourself is to surrender at God's feet and be ready to go on a new adventure of discovery with God as you navigate the waters of issues of life as they come up. There are practical tips of how to come back from a setback to not just pick the pieces but run with fresh visions. We will be learning from our Master Jesus as He held on to the vision of the salvation of humanity through His death on the cross of calvary. The secret of His staying power in the face of obvious pressures in the pursuit of the mission of saving mankind would be so instructive to you as you go through your own daily pressures. It is hoped that you will feel empowered to win your way through the dark cloudy storms. The vision will come to pass by God's help as you hold on to it firmly to the very end. **Habakuk 2:3**

DEDICATION

This book is dedicated to the Almighty God, my author and finisher, the glory, and the lifter up of my head. He remains my unending source of inspiration, grace, favour, and strength in whom I live and move and have my being.

I dedicate this book to my dear wife Olabisi whom the Lord brought alongside me on my journey in life as a true companion as we patiently waited for our time to come. It is divinely decreed that both as individuals and as a family, we all will continually reap the fruits of our labour. Together we will enjoy unending seasons of break forth and breakthroughs in all dimensions of life as the Lord lives Amen.

This work is also dedicated to my lovely princesses; Boluwatife, Inioluwa and Ewaoluwa who remain 'choice children of God' who have encouraged me along the way. I dedicate this work similarly to the multitudes out there who are hungry to fulfil the purpose for which God created them having come to a place where they are no longer satisfied with anything less. I want to assure you that in the name of Jesus your time will surely come to be celebrated, congratulated, favoured, and blessed in the due season of your life as you gain insight from the pages of this book.

INTRODUCTION

L ife in general and how you live it is all about the vision you
have in the first place, everything we see including the work of
creation springs from a vision.
So what then is vision?
This is the unseen blueprint of a potential future which guides you as
a person on how to optimise the opportunities that come your way to
align to the blueprint in the mind. Whenever there is a lack of vision,
waste and mismanagement of opportunities will be rife. The result of
cause would be a non-fulfilment of purpose and a great under
performance of your capacity to perform.

Vision would preserve you even during the worst level of decadence
around you, it was vision that ensured that Daniel was not corrupted
in Babylon. Similarly, vision keep Isaac sowing in the land even
through a national season of famine, in the end, Isaac got a bountiful
harvest while his contemporaries got none because in their lacking
vision, they did not sow seed when Isaac did. The vision you have
must however be driven by your faith in God as a believer, the wise
words of scripture acting as an unending source of fuel to propel you
on your journey of unlimited success and excellence where you
outperform all others.

The patriarchs of old used it to prepare their route to prevailing
success even in a complicated world not too dis-similar to the one
you and I are in today, it helped them through their issues and
without any doubt it will help you too today. This book will expose

you to time-tested principles applicable across a range of situations that will make you always a winner no matter what life throws at you. Its pages will both inspire and challenge you to go further faster than you have ever done before in the pursuit of enduring excellence as you take the lessons to heart.

It is hoped that the careful outlining of the vision will not just guide you but guide your generation to the path of incredible achievements all the time notwithstanding the obstacles you face. Lessons are drawn from well known as well as some obscure biblical characters to bolster your faith and give you an edge over your competitors. I trust God to meet you through this work and make you fulfil all your potentials exponentially.

WHAT VISION ARE YOU SEEING?
Genesis 13:14-15

In a nutshell, a vision is a roadmap, insight or blueprint into the potential future that can be for an individual, group, organisation, or a people. It provides a guide into your ordained purpose to direct you to the expected destination in life. Without a vision, you run the risk of languishing in inactivity and marooning your destiny on the shores of failure. Where vision is lacking, waste of resources and opportunities occurs at all levels. The Almighty God demonstrated the importance and the power of visions to turn a catastrophic disaster into what today is a resounding emphatic enduring breakthrough that perpetually frustrates the plans the devil had in destroying creation. The vision of God amid the chaos caused by the devil as he attacked the earth God created led to a visionary recreation of a destroyed creation.

1 In the beginning God created the heavens and the earth. 2 The earth was without form, and void; and darkness was on the face of the deep. And the Spirit of God was hovering over the face of the waters. 3 Then God said, "Let there be light"; and there was light.
Genesis 1:1-3

Therefore rejoice, O heavens, and you who dwell in them! Woe to the inhabitants of the earth and the sea! For the devil has come *down to you, having great wrath, because he knows that he has a short time." **Revelation 12:12***

Vision equipped God to thwart the 3-point agenda of the devil for humanity that remains to steal, kill and destroy everything good, and blessings ordained for humanity by God from the very foundation of the earth. This great resource of the divine vision imprinted on God's heart ultimately enabled God to fully repurpose things to align with His original programme for the world **Genesis 1:4-31.**

How do you obtain a 'God -given vision' for your life?
Look away from yourself with all the inadequacies or limitations that have come into your life from either nature or nurture around you, look unto God for guidance to get into your next level of fulfilment. Do not limit your options and plans to the current level of your understanding, look up to God for fresh inspirations to greater heights.

*Trust in the Lord with all your heart and lean not on your own understanding; 6 In all your ways acknowledge Him, And He shall direct your paths.***Proverbs 3:5-8**

Abram obtained guidance from the Almighty God to see beyond what was right before him at a very crucial time of his life just after Lot left him unexpectedly after a long season of strife between their two families as uncle and nephew. Spend time away from all sources of distractions alone with God who is often heard and experienced in the place of quiet focus and contemplation when you intentionally seek Him.

I will stand my watch. And set myself on the rampart and watch to see what He will say to me, and what I will answer when I am corrected. **Habakkuk 2:1**.

To encounter God is to obtain a fresh vision that will renew your focus and set you aflame again in the pursuit of purpose. Just as we see in the life of the prophet Elijah, to get a divine encounter you must wait patiently to seek it when God chooses to show up.

8 So he arose and ate and drank; and he went in the strength of that food forty days and forty nights as far as Horeb, the mountain of God. 9 And there he went into a cave, and spent the night in that place; and behold, the word of the Lord came to him, and He said to him, "What are you doing here, Elijah?" **1 Kings 19:8-9**

Keep the door of your heart open to God, the all-knowing God would like to dialogue with you and reveal mysteries to you if you give Him room in your heartwhen He knocks. There is so much He would like to share with you if only you can create the time to hear Him.

20 Behold, I stand at the door and knock. If anyone hears My voice and opens the door, I will come into him and dine with him, and he with Me. 21 To him who overcomes I will grant to sit with Me on My throne, as I also overcame and sat down with My Father on His throne. **Revelation 3:20-21**.

It is God's delight to provide you clear detailed guidance through His Spirit that He pours out upon His own children who will be eager to receive the awesome presence of God. Do not let God have to back you into a corner and break down your resistance to His will and purposes, let your heart be a fertile ground for God to sow in fresh visions of your glorious future in Him as you commune with God as a child of God to a loving heavenly Father.

18 "Come now, and let us reason together," Says the Lord, "Though your sins are like scarlet, they shall be as white as snow; Though they are red like crimson, they shall be as wool. 19 If you are willing and obedient, you shall eat the good of the land; 20 But if you refuse and rebel, you shall be devoured by the sword"; For the mouth of the Lord has spoken. **Isaiah 1:18-20**

Considering the way, the Lord dealt with Abram who questioned the revelations of the purpose of God and demanded proof of God's ability to perform it, Abram was encouraged to have a dialogue and seek clarification of the future as he came in the place of intimacy with God in the secret place of prayer under guarded by his lavish sacrifice to the Almighty God. In the same way, God wants to fellowship with you to give you a new vision of what your tomorrow will be if only you spend time alone with Him.

8 And he said, "Lord God, how shall I know that I will inherit it?" 9 So He said to him, "Bring Me a three-year-old heifer, a three-year-old female goat, a three-year-old ram, a turtledove, and a young pigeon." 10 Then he brought all these to Him and cut them in two, down the middle, and placed each piece opposite the other; but he did not cut the birds in two. 11 And when the vultures came down on the carcasses, Abram drove them away. 12 Now when the sun was going down, a deep sleep fell upon Abram; and behold, horror and great darkness fell upon him. 13 Then He said to Abram: "Know certainly that your descendants will be strangers in a land that is not theirs, and will serve them, and they will afflict them four hundred years. 14 And also the nation whom they serve I will judge; afterward they shall come out with great possessions. 15 Now as for you, you shall go to your fathers in peace; you shall be buried at a good old age. 16 But in the fourth generation they shall return here, for the iniquity of the Amorites is not yet complete." 17 And it came to pass, when the sun went down and it was dark, that behold, there appeared a smoking oven and a burning torch that passed between those pieces. 18 On the same day the Lord made a covenant with Abram, saying: "To your descendants I have given this land, from the river of Egypt to the great river, the river Euphrates—**Genesis 15:8-18**

Get familiar with God's thinking as found in the various pages of the Holy scriptures, love His words, and keep them in your heart, these would be a catalyst to inspire fresh visions when you fellowship with God alone.

Conclusion
Walk with God in a love relationship so His Spirit flows through you like a spring of righteousness. God's spirit is willing to flow in fresh visions through you as you seek Him sincerely.

37 On the last day, that great day of the feast, Jesus stood and cried out, saying, "If anyone thirsts, let him come to Me and drink. 38 He who believes in Me, as the Scripture has said, out of his heart will *flow rivers of living water." **39** But this He spoke concerning the Spirit, whom those believing in Him would receive; for the Holy Spirit was not yet given, because Jesus was not yet glorified.* **John 7:37-39**

DESPISE NOT PROPHESY!
1 Thessalonians 5:20-21

W hat is a prophecy from the Christian perspective? It is a divinely inspired word given to God's appointed vessel to reveal or proclaim an inspired vision, blueprint, insight, or timeline of events that have been ordained to take place. There is no divine prophecy that originates from a personal private manufacture or fabrications from the minds of a person's thoughts or imaginations, rather it is God's vision implanted into your heart by the outpouring of God's Holy Spirit upon your heart.

*20 knowing this first, that no prophecy of Scripture is of any private interpretation, 21 for prophecy never came by the will of man, but holy men of God spoke as they were moved by the Holy Spirit.*2 **Peter 1:20-21**

"And it shall come to pass afterward that I will pour out My Spirit on all flesh; Your sons and your daughters shall prophesy, your old men shall dream dreams, Your young men shall see visions. **Joel 2:28**

God's Spirit at work in your heart that you have opened to Him will inspire you to proclaim God's vision at such a time as this. The divine inspiration will be dynamic, full of the word of wisdom (full of inspiration on the wise use of scriptures in the situation) and the word of knowledge (full of clear information to help you make informed choices or opinions on an unclear matter) as the Lord gives utterance.

for one is given the word of wisdom through the Spirit, to another the word of knowledge through the same Spirit, **1 Corinthians 12:8.**

To engage with prophesy, you must believe in God who sent them, and you shall be established in truth, also believe the prophetic vessels He sent the words through so that you shall surely prosper against all odds as the Almighty God steps in to do what is humanly impossible to accomplish.

So, they rose early in the morning and went out into the Wilderness of Tekoa; and as they went out, Jehoshaphat stood and said, "Hear me, O Judah and you inhabitants of Jerusalem: Believe in the Lord your God, and you shall be established; believe His prophets, and you shall prosper." **2 Chronicles 20:20**

Are you facing an impossible situation right now? Go into the presence of God and obtain a prophetic word from the Holy Spirit to create a new reality to the glory and praise of God. You will have a new song of uncommon unconventional victory through Christ at work.

A case study - the doubting leader
1 Then Elisha said, "Hear the word of the Lord. Thus says the Lord: 'Tomorrow about this time a seah of fine flour shall be sold for a shekel, and two seahs of barley for a shekel, at the gate of Samaria.' " 2 So an officer on whose hand the king leaned answered the man of God and said, "Look, if the Lord would make windows in heaven, could this thing be?" And he said, "In fact, you shall see it with your eyes, but you shall not eat of it." **2 Kings 7:1-2**

Put this bible account of what took place into context. Currently in our world, the financial indices of the various economies of the world means that the interest rates of most countries are on the high side. Added to these pressures are the various local situations that have been created by global geo-political tensions, climate change, new post pandemic changes that have changed the global markets profoundly. Could you imagine someone coming up to predict that within twenty- four hours or less, all these problems would vanish, and things would become better at all levels similarly to how the economy was booming before things took a tumble for the worst. I bet practically everyone would call such an individual deranged. However, when you are dealing with God, the spiritual realm of divinely inspired prophecy can transform things overnight.

Many years ago, I was directed by the Holy Spirit to be a part of a church ministry in one of the countries of Africa that was clearly struggling to survive. I was a fresh graduate of engineering returning from my service year when the Spirit of God impressed on me to join this ministry.

A brief description of the structure where the services took place for the benefit of those who might never have come across such buildings is a hall that had corrugated iron sheets for a roof supported by dozens of 8-foot wooden posts installed into the ground covered with orange clay laterite soil. Around this was about three to four brick high walls to mark the outline of the hall. The floor was dusty, the seats were made from 3 metres long wooden planks supported intermittently by wooden supports for legs to make benches for the congregation to sit on. These benches had been so badly impacted by the hot sun beaming down on them from an uninsulated roof that they had begun to warp out of shape and had become very unstable. To say the ministry was suffering from chronic lack of funding was an understatement. If it were up to me, I certainly would not have chosen or even considered it a place to serve God.

After joining the ministry, I remember vividly one day after a session of prayer that the Lord brought a vision to my heart and began to prophesy through me calling forth doors, windows, roof ceiling, walls, chairs, equipment, the pastor's office and much more. At the time this was going on, it just seemed totally impossible because the membership of the church were mostly petty traders who were below average income earners and the funds needed to bring these into being were quite phenomenal but as God usually does, He brought about the change soon after. Someone joined the church and just took an interest in developing the premises in line with what had been prophesied.

Going back now to our bible story, a prominent and highly visible leadership figure in the nation of Israel at that time who was highly respected as well as a leader that commanded a following among the people was a spiritual sceptic who swayed the opinion of many away from truth despite a clear track record of outstanding performance of God's words through the prophet.

18 So when the Syrians came down to him, Elisha prayed to the Lord, and said, "Strike this people, I pray, with blindness." And He struck them with blindness according to the word of Elisha. 19 Now Elisha said to them, "This is not the way, nor is this the city. Follow me, and I will bring you to the man whom you seek." But he led them to Samaria. 20 So it was, when they had come to Samaria, that Elisha said, "Lord, open the eyes of these men, that they may see." And the Lord opened their eyes, and they saw; and there they were, inside Samaria! 21 Now when the king of Israel saw them, he said to Elisha, "My father, shall I kill them? Shall I kill them?" 22 But he answered, "You shall not kill them. Would you kill those whom you have taken captive with your sword and your bow? Set food and water before them, so that they may eat and drink and go to their master." 23 Then he prepared a great feast for them; and after they ate and drank, he sent them away and they went to their master. So, the bands of Syrian raiders came no more into the land of Israel. 2 **Kings 6:18-23**

This prominent aide to the King wanted to weaken the faith of many by ridiculing the words of the Prophet just like Sanballat and Tobias did when the broken-down walls of Jerusalem were being rebuilt.

1 But it so happened, when Sanballat heard that we were rebuilding the wall, that he was furious and very indignant, and mocked the Jews. 2 And he spoke before his brethren and the army of Samaria, and said, "What are these feeble Jews doing? Will they fortify themselves? Will they offer sacrifices? Will they complete it in a day? Will they revive the stones from the heaps of rubbish—stones that are burned?" 3 Now Tobiah the Ammonite was beside him, and he said, "Whatever they build, if even a fox goes up on it, he will break down their stone wall." 4 Hear, O our God, for we are despised; turn their reproach on their own heads, and give them as plunder to a land of captivity! **Nehemiah 4:1-4**

Do not copy this bad example or engage in making mockery of the efforts of others who are doing the work of God as inspired by the Holy Spirit, this could have horrible unintended consequences which you might regret.

The ploy of this high ranking official in the nation of Israel to court influence over the King and the people as an opinion leader however backfired spectacularly. As the prophecy was being fulfilled in his very presence, he saw it happen but as had been prophesied against him as a judgement for his mockery of God, he did not get any benefit from the manifestation of the prophecy.

16 Then the people went out and plundered the tents of the Syrians. So, a seah of fine flour was sold for a shekel, and two seahs of barley for a shekel, according to the word of the Lord. 17 Now the king had appointed the officer on whose hand he leaned on to take charge of the gate. But the people trampled him in the gate, and he died, just as the man of God had said, who spoke when the king came down to him. **2 Kings 7:16-17**

Conclusion

Are you a non - believer in God, come now to the Almighty. Are you a sceptic or one who has been misguided by someone walking in the way of error as dictated by their proud or arrogant heart, come now to God. Are you hurting now from a previous painful encounter with the practice of faith which has turned you off believing in prophecy, come now, God is inviting you.

8 Come to Me, all you who labour and are heavy laden, and I will give you rest. 29 Take My yoke upon you and learn from Me, for I am gentle and lowly in heart, and you will find rest for your souls. 30 For My yoke is easy and My burden is light." **Matthew 11:28-30**

It is a new season; it is a new day for you to obtain a new glorious spiritual vision to take you to where God has ordained for you to be.

VISION OF A HARVEST
John 4:34-35

V ision and times or seasons of life will happen to everyone
irrespective of who or where you are located on the surface of the
earth. These two forces operate in tandem with one another. This is
illustrated by the fact that what you pursue at every stage of life is in
line with the time and the specific season you find yourself at that
moment in time. So as a child under the age of 15, your dreams,
desires, goals and aspirations which together form your vision are
limited to the thing's teenagers within the context of your cultural
exposure around you want.
There is the natural time and season of life which defines what
happens to you at that phase of life. Consequently, when the harvest
of life comes in accordance with natural laws of nature, it is within
what is expected of life at this phase of existence as would
commonly happen to anyone on average naturally speaking.

*To everything there is a season, A time for every purpose under
heaven:* **Ecclesiastes 3:1.**

There is also, however, a supernatural controlled time and season of
life orchestrated by God that supersedes the natural laws of nature in
determining the time and speed of your harvest season. This operates
outside the natural laws of nature or time and chance that happens to
everyone. It is an exclusive privilege of those who have put their
trust in the Almighty God and often always supersedes the natural

expectations buoyed on the wings of firm faith or belief in the provisions of the eternal promises of God to you.

He has made everything beautiful in its time. Also, He has put eternity in their hearts, except that no one can find out the work that God does from beginning to end. **Ecclesiastes 3:11**

You must always tune into this supernatural vision of a harvest season as you serve and apply scriptural principles or practices that provoke a response from Heaven. The implication of this is that in everything you do, you must always have the harvest in mind because you understand that there is nothing you do that is in vain or without a harvest that will surely come to you sooner or later in your life. Once you allow yourself to be driven by the vision of a harvest to come for every effort you put in, the incentive will always be there for you to do your best at every opportunity, you can't tell which effort will be ripe for a harvest.

5 As you do not know what the way of the wind is, or how the bones grow in the womb of her who is with child, so you do not know the works of God who makes everything. 6 In the morning sow your seed, and in the evening do not withhold your hand; For you do not know which will prosper, either this or that, or whether both alike will be good. **Ecclesiastes 11:5-6**

Focus your energy therefore on fulfilling God's purpose for your existence as you daily run your race, this will guarantee an alignment to God's supernatural provision of resources. The divine supply of grace and open heavens into your life to help you fully complete God's purposes. Creativity flows when you see with the eye of imaginative faith a harvest even before you see or consider the obstacles ahead of you. A release from on high opens the supernatural provisions of God to you to tap into for phenomenal performance.

I can do all things through Christ who strengthens me. **Philippians 4:13**

Commit to do everything as God's ambassadors to walk in faith trusting to see the vision of a harvest right at the point of the release of the 'seed of commitment to that purpose' you engage in by faith.

*For in it the righteousness of God is revealed from faith to faith; as it is written, "The just shall live by faith."***Romans 1:17**

Just like God would, you should see the vision of a great end from the beginning, what you see shall come to pass! All things are possible to you if you have faith. Things will always work for you according to your level of faith that it would happen as you have spoken.

*Then He touched their eyes, saying, "According to your faith let it be to you."***Matthew 9:29**

With your empathic vision of faith, your harvest can be brought forward supernaturally out of the realm of the natural speed of things at God's uncommon speed. Your harvest is here!

Conclusion
You shall have what you ask for and proclaim in the place of prayer notwithstanding how improbable it might seem; we have the mandate to subdue mountains and obstacles by exercising our unmitigated faith in God's words and promises to us.

Therefore, I say to you, whatever things you ask when you pray, believe that you receive *them,* and you will have *them.* **Mark 11:24**

Jesus demonstrated how this will come to pass and He is on the inside of you if you are a believer. There is no limit or realm that the power of faith in the harvest that is firmly based on your unshakable belief in God cannot penetrate.

39 Jesus said, "Take away the stone."Martha, the sister of him who was dead, said to Him, "Lord, by this time there is a stench, for he has been dead for four days." 40 Jesus said to her, "Did I not say to you that if you would believe you would see the glory of God?" 41 Then they took away the stone from the place where the dead man was lying. And Jesus lifted up His eyes and said, "Father, I thank

You that You have heard Me. 42 And I know that You always hear Me, but because of the people who are standing by I said this, that they may believe that You sent Me." 43 Now when He had said these things, He cried with a loud voice, "Lazarus, come forth!" 44 And he who had died came out bound hand and foot with graveclothes, and his face was wrapped with a cloth. Jesus said to them, "Loose him, and let him go." **John 11:39-44**

The only people who this would not work for are the unsaved who have no faith or belief in God's atoning sacrifice for their lives. God is inviting you to come to Him today to obtain your divinely allocated harvest. Are you battling with difficulties, challenges and never seeming to be able to overcome them? God is inviting you to bring them to Him, today is an opportunity to exchange your difficulties for a harvest of divine rest in God. Would you respond to the invitation from God directly to you today?

28 Come to Me, all you who labour and are heavy laden, and I will give you rest. 29 Take My yoke upon you and learn from Me, for I am gentle and lowly in heart, and you will find rest for your souls. 30 For My yoke is easy and My burden is light." **Matthew 11:28-30.**

WHY SIT HERE AND DIE?
2 Kings 7:3-10

T he unique ability to question your situations and
circumstances in the light of God's purposes for your life is essential
to break free from all forms of limitations or stagnations that hinder
us from soaring in life. Every move we make as people who are
regenerated in their minds comes from our 'divinely renewed mind'
which is engaged in thinking scripturally without constraints or
restraints to views that are contrary to our faith in God. As far as the
Kingdom of Heaven is concerned, everything becomes possible in
the Spiritual realm and then translates into the physical realm.

*Jesus said to him, "If you can believe, all things are possible to him
who believes."*
Mark 9:23

God chose to elevate 4 lepers who were the lowest in society cadre.
They were greatly hated, ostracised, and most often ignored in the
community yet God was determined to make them intergenerational
celebrities of all times. Are you in a similar situation today, I want to
tell you that you are next in line!

*26 For you see your calling, brethren, that not many wise according
to the flesh, not many mighty, not many noble, are called. 27 But
God has chosen the foolish things of the world to put to shame the
wise, and God has chosen the weak things of the world to put to
shame the things which are mighty; 28 and the base things of the*

world and the things which are despised God has chosen, and the things which are not, to bring to nothing the things that are, **1 Corinthians 1:26-28.**

Life presents to you as a person, opportunities wrapped in the catalyst of problems specifically designed by God to bring you out of obscurity and launch you into prominence. These specific sets of obstacles are designed to stretch your potential to bring out the very best version of you into manifestation even though it often does not seem to be so when you encounter them.

*Then your light shall break forth like the morning, your healing shall spring forth speedily, and your righteousness shall go before you; The glory of the Lord shall be your rear guard.***Isaiah 58:8**

Goliath revealed David, the unusual famine in Egypt launched the career of Joseph as an outstanding Prime Minister of all times, the unjust laws of Babylon against the Jews brought out the star of Esther which outshone every darkness in the kingdom of Babylon in her days. The heavy persecutions against believers made Paul an acclaimed global evangelist.
What is the problem God has allowed to come your way? Arise and solve it swiftly in the power of God, do not delay your shining, it is only the living that can make history not the dead! Redeem the time bound opportunity that God has sent your way beloved. Take note that the doors of opportunities to advance or move ahead of your contemporaries never remain open or available to you forever especially if you do not engage with them. Put your very best into whatever you have access to, this was the resolve of the four lepers.

*Whatever your hand finds to do, do it with all your might; for there is no work or device or knowledge or wisdom in the grave where you are going.***Ecclesiastes 9:10**

The problem you solve by God's help will bring you uncommon glory globally.
Develop a possibility mentality modelled after the life and example of Jesus Christ.There is a cloud of Witness watching you and your every move, these are made up of challenges, detractors, speculators,

supporters, enemies, friends, issues of life that challenges your vision of life. These and many more are the constant clouds of Witness that are around you are watching your every move. These should be sources of catalytic motivations to spur you on to exert yourself to ensure you excel above all others irrespective of what cards life delves to you.

1 Therefore we also, since we are surrounded by so great a cloud of witnesses, let us lay aside every weight, and the sin which so easily ensnares us, and let us run with endurance the race that is set before us, 2 looking unto Jesus, the author and finisher of our faith, who for the joy that was set before Him endured the cross, despising the shame, and has sat down at the right hand of the throne of God. **Hebrews 12:1-2**

Don't be complacent or satisfied with the accolades and successes of the past victories, seize the moment, take the risk, and put what you have available to you to use. Today is another opportunity to press into another level, you are not there yet, keep pressing on.

Not that I have already attained, or am already perfected; but I press on, that I may lay hold of that for which Christ Jesus has also laid hold of me. **Philippians 3:14**

Woe to you who are at ease in Zion, and trust in Mount Samaria, Notable persons in the chief nation, to whom the house of Israel comes! **Amos 6:1**

Avoid like a plague the spirit of average effort which is the 'worst of the best and the best of the worst'. The man Lot in the bible fell victim to 'the spirit of average syndrome' This was a very costly mistake that cost Lot and his family their future. It was in the place Lot chose to stay with his two daughters against divine instruction that was eventually where he compromised so badly that he ended up having incestual relationships with them. Lot lost everything in his future because of compromise and modulation of the directives of God to him.

See now, this city is near enough to flee to, and it is a little one; please let me escape there (is it not a little one?) and my soul shall live."**Genesis 19:20**

Sacrifice your views, hopes, fears, apprehensions, plans just as those four lepers did in response to the inner nudging of God's spirit in their heart on the altar of total obedience to God always. The four lepers did what they could do, and they did it so well that God amplified their efforts. The opposition heard a sound like that of a mighty army on approach, they rose and fled without waiting to pick anything that was precious or useful to them. What the Lord did in the lives of these lepers, the Almighty God can do in your life if you give Him the space and room for this.

Ask yourself very key questions based on your faith and renewed mind in Christ not on the worldly, ungodly views prevalent around you. Do not be cowardly or afraid to go against all human logic as you free your mind of all the limitations which the surrounding situations and circumstances place on it! This simple act of faith unlocks your potentials to encounter the contributions of God that will guarantee total victories.

3 Now there were four leprous men at the entrance of the gate; and they said to one another, "Why are we sitting here until we die? 4 If we say, 'We will enter the city,' the famine is in the city, and we shall die there. And if we sit here, we die also. Now therefore, come, let us surrender to the army of the Syrians. If they keep us alive, we shall live; and if they kill us, we shall only die." **2 Kings 7: 3-4**

Uncommon victories, miracles, great unheard-of testimonies are for those who are willing to take a risk on their faith by acting out what they believe, or hope would happen. The greatest tragedy is the great losses we experience simply because we do not want to step out of our comfort zone in life. If you are comfortable with the issues around your life in this comfort zone, nothing will ever change! For the believer in Christ Jesus, your bold faith in His words is the ever-available catalyst of change that births fantastic testimonies for you and those around you.

But without faith it is impossible to please Him, for he who comes to God must believe that He is, and that He is a rewarder of those who diligently seek Him. **Hebrews 11:6**

Be of good courage, And He shall strengthen your heart, All you who hope in the Lord. **Psalm 31:24**

Remember, God is going before you always to make all the obstacles and barriers to your miracle collapse before you as you make a move of faith, if you do not move, God will stop too until you are ready to advance forward. God cannot go beyond your choice lest He overrides your self will, you must do what you can do to allow God to do what you cannot do as He promised.

"Behold, I send an Angel before you to keep you in the way and to bring you into the place which I have prepared. **Exodus 23:20**

*And the Lord your God will expel them from before you and drive them out of your sight. So, you shall possess their land, as the Lord your God promised you.***Joshua 23:5**

However, just like the four lepers, you must keep advancing forward in your pursuit, this enables God to amplify and magnify the place of your feet underneath you to set you up for phenomenal victorious breakthroughs. The Lord went ahead of the lepers into the enemy camp and drove the Syrian army out of the place before the lepers got there just as the lepers started their own journey to the camp!

5 And they rose at **twilight** *to go to the camp of the Syrians; and when they had come to the outskirts of the Syrian camp, to their surprise no one was there. 6 For the Lord had caused the army of the Syrians to hear the noise of chariots and the noise of horses—the noise of a great army; so they said to one another, "Look, the king of Israel has hired against us the kings of the Hittites and the kings of the Egyptians to attack us!" 7 Therefore they arose and fled at* **twilight***, and left the camp intact—their tents, their horses, and their donkeys—and they fled for their lives. 8 And when these lepers came to the outskirts of the camp, they went into one tent and ate and drank, and carried from it silver and gold and clothing, and went* *and hid them; then they came back and entered another tent, and carried some from there also, and went and hid it.* **2 Kings 7:5-8**

If you stop, God will pause your victory.

*27 "I will send My fear before you, I will cause confusion among all the people to whom you come and will make all your enemies turn their backs to you. 28 And I will send hornets before you, which shall drive out the Hivite, the Canaanite, and the Hittite from before you. 29 I will not drive them out from before you in one year, lest the land become desolate, and the beasts of the field become too numerous for you. 30 Little by little I will drive them out from before you, until you have increased, and you inherit the land.***Exodus 23:27-30**

Conclusion

You are God's instrument of glory in these times you are living in, the Almighty God will magnify you in your generation, arise dear battle-axe of the Lord, God has need of you right now, what are you waiting for? Why sit where you are? Go forward in His power now.

For the eyes of the Lord run to and fro throughout the whole earth, to show Himself strong on behalf of those whose heart is loyal to Him. In this you have done foolishly, therefore from now on you shall have wars." **2 Chronicles 16:9**

*"You are My battle-axe and weapons of war: For with you I will break the nation in pieces; With you I will destroy kingdoms;***Jeremiah 51:20**.

GO AGAIN SEVEN TIMES
1 Kings 18: 43-44

G od is the key determinant of your times and seasons in life irrespective of how things look in the physical realm. The Almighty God is always in control in line with His divine agenda ordained for your life from the very foundation of the earth.

Known to God from eternity are all His works **Acts 15:18**.

You and your life's situation are God's platform to glorify Himself in your life, your life situation is a display board to showcase the unlimited ability of God to make something great out of a wrecked or damaged life.

17 that Christ may dwell in your hearts through faith; that you, being rooted and grounded in love, 18 may be able to comprehend with all the saints what is the width and lengthand depth and height— 19 to know the love of Christ which passes knowledge; that you may be filled with all the fullness of God. 20 Now to Him who can do exceedingly abundantly above all that we ask or think, according to the power that works in us, 21 to Him be glory in the church by Christ Jesus to all generations, forever and ever. Amen. **Ephesians 3:17-21**

God will keep on working things out until you fully enter and experience divine plan for your life.
There is a perfect time for your miracle, keep your focus on God rather than the prevailing circumstances, you will see His glory

breakthrough at the time divinely appointed for it. You might have to look again, pray again, go again, try again even seven times to arrive at your miracle destination but the breakthrough will happen only do not give up!

He has made everything beautiful in its time. Also, He has put eternity in their hearts, except that no one can find out the work that God does from beginning to end. **Ecclesiastes 3:11**

43 and said to his servant, "Go up now, look toward the sea." So, he went up and looked, and said, *"There is* nothing." And seven times he said, "Go again." **44** Then it came to pass the seventh *time,* that he said, "There is a cloud, as small as a man's hand, rising out of the sea!" So, he said, "Go up, say to Ahab, 'Prepare *your chariot,* and go down before the rain stops you.'" **1 Kings 18:43-44.**

Case study -The enemy ambush

15 And when the servant of the man of God arose early and went out, there was an army, surrounding the city with horses and chariots. And his servant said to him, "Alas, my master! What shall we do?" 16 So he answered, "Do not fear, for those who are with us are more than those who are with them." 17 And Elisha prayed, and said, "Lord, I pray, open his eyes that he may see." Then the Lord opened the eyes of the young man, and he saw. And behold, the mountain was full of horses and chariots of fire all around Elisha.2 **Kings 6:15-17**

Elisha's servant initially saw certain defeat and total annihilation at the hands of the great enemy that surrounded them unexpectedly. Although they often say, first impressions last longer, in this context the initial situation of things did not last because God had not yet stepped into the situation. Whatever the situation is looking like right now for you, don't conclude that it is all over, the Almighty God can still make a difference. Looking through the eye of faith, when the servant looked again at the word of his master Elisha the prophet, he saw victory and divine supply instead of destruction. Look again!

Jesus Christ mentored us in the school of going again until you obtain the victory promised to you as recorded in the scriptures. To see again by faith, get rid of every weight or obstacles to your seeing the situation by faith, view the situation from a spiritual perspective.

1 Therefore we also, since we are surrounded by so great a cloud of witnesses, let us lay aside every weight, and the sin which so easily ensnares us, and let us run with endurance the race that is set before us, 2 looking unto Jesus, the author and finisher of our faith, who for the joy that was set before Him endured the cross, despising the shame, and has sat down at the right hand of the throne of God. 3 For consider Him who endured such hostility from sinners against Himself, lest you become weary and discouraged in your souls.
Hebrews 12:1-3

The joy of victory possible when we see the situation by faith made Jesus engage in intense prayers again and again until the victory was obtained in the spirit realm of prayers. Like Jesus, keep going again and again in the place of prayers to possess your allocated miraculous breakthroughs that will make your joy complete. If Jesus prayed again and again and again until victory came, you too must be going again and again until you get yours too!

32 Then they came to a place which was named Gethsemane; and He said to His disciples, "Sit here while I pray." 33 And He took Peter, James, and John with Him, and He began to be troubled and deeply distressed. 34 Then He said to them, "My soul is exceedingly sorrowful, even to death. Stay here and watch." 35 He went a little farther, and fell on the ground, and prayed that if it were possible, the hour might pass from Him. 36 And He said, "Abba, Father, all things are possible for You. Take this cup away from Me; nevertheless, not what I will, but what You will." 37 Then He came and found them sleeping, and said to Peter, "Simon, are you sleeping? Could you not watch one hour? 38 Watch and pray, lest you enter temptation. The spirit indeed is willing, but the flesh is weak." 39 Again He went away and prayed and spoke the same words. 40 And when He returned, He found them asleep again, for their eyes were heavy; and they did not know what to answer Him.

41 Then He came the third time and said to them, "Are you still sleeping and resting? It is enough! The hour has come; behold, the Son of Man is being betrayed into the hands of sinners. 42 Rise, let us be going. See, my betrayer is at hand." **Mark 14:32-42**

The bigger the miracle you demand for, the bigger your prayers to the Almighty God must be. The more glorious the testimony you are expecting, the bigger your 'faith-o-meter' must be too! Check out the prayer intensity of Jesus who was in the most critical season of HIs life in the phase of the fulfilment of the destiny assignment of salvation of humanity. Jesus prayed for three hours straight, praying again and again. What then is your excuse for stopping your prayers?

38 Then He said to them, "My soul is exceedingly sorrowful, even to death. Stay here and watch with Me." 39 He went a little farther and fell on His face, and prayed, saying, "O My Father, if it is possible, let this cup pass from Me; nevertheless, not as I will, but as You will." 40 Then He came to the disciples and found them sleeping, and said to Peter, "What! Could you not watch with Me for one hour? 41 Watch and pray, lest you enter temptation. The spirit indeed is willing, but the flesh is weak." 42 Again, a second time, He went away and prayed, saying, "O My Father, if this cup cannot pass away from Me unless I drink it, Your will be done." 43 And He came and found them asleep again, for their eyes were heavy. 44 So He left them, went away again, and prayed the third time, saying the same words. **Matthew 26:38-44**.

Remember at the time Jesus prayed, everything had been given unto His hands. Jesus had had supernatural encounters in the supernatural realms that fully manifested in the physical realms, yet He prayed again and again.

Jesus, knowing that the Father had given all things into His hands, and that He had come from God and was going to God. **John 13:3**

Conclusion
Keep praying until you break through into your joy, there is a seventh time for the perfection of your miracle in your own fullness

of time, it is not too late to pray God's vision for your life through **Luke 1:57 (5-21)** if only you believe in God, you will see His Glory.

Jesus said to her, "Did I not say to you that if you would believe you would see the glory of God?" **John 11:40**

PREVAILING VISION OF VICTORY

1 Samuel 17:33-37

In life, there are two doors open to all humanity that always exist as options for each of us to walk into at any point in time, each of these doors will lead to different outcomes. The first door is called **'I Can'** and it is an expression of positive ability in the effort we can put into a venture or pursuit. The other counterpart door is the door of **'I Cannot'** which is an expression of negative inability or the non-belief in one's capability of achieving any desired outcome from the investment of time or resources committed to a venture pursued.

It is to be noted that 'I cannot' could also be an expression of positive ability or believing faith for example, you could live by the philosophy that because God reigns in your life, you 'cannot fail. In this instance, there is an element of positive discrimination.

The door you chose to subscribe to is hugely dependent on our overriding vision that you have chosen to be guided by and which we actively pursue. The proof of our faith in God is in the subsequent actions you take in line with the faith you have.

For as the body without the spirit is dead, so faith without works is dead also. **James 2:26**

An illustration of this principle is demonstrated by the example of the young boy David as he confronted the giant Goliath who was in every way bigger and more experienced on the battlefield. Buoyed by the deep faith David had in the living God's ability to help him conquer Goliath just as this same God had helped him overcome the lion and the bear that threatened his sheep in the wilderness, David ran enthusiastically towards Goliath on the day of battle.

*So it was, when the Philistine arose and came and drew near to meet David, that David hurried and ran toward the army to meet the Philistine.***1 Samuel 17:48**

The vision of victory in the face of obvious defeat motivated David to eagerly run to clash and overcome the obstacle that was before him. Every option of defeat or retreat was blocked out of his mind, only one outcome was entertained in his thoughts and imaginations, this was the sure defeat of goliath by the encompassing power of the Almighty God that never loses a battle!

Keep hold of your vision that you have become persuaded of in God as the guiding light for your journey in life, do all you can to avoid 'negative vision peddlers' who are there to dissuade you from your destiny journey.

Many years ago, when we needed to move from our cramped one-bedroom flat to ensure appropriate accommodation for our expanding family, my wife and I went to a financial adviser to explore options of getting a mortgage for our own house. We gave the finance professional all the necessary details of our income and outgoings as well as the prospects for the future to analyse and give us advice. The outcome was not encouraging at all, based on the single income that was coming into the family at that time, there was no prospect of getting a mortgage without some help. Following this consultation, we left the adviser discouraged by what He had said but still confident that the Almighty God would help us one way or the other.

This vision that there would be a way made us continue to explore possibilities. We keep looking for a way that this vision of getting our own home would become a possibility even as we believed in the word of the Almighty God above the negative prognosis of the financial adviser. Because we were looking, the Lord enabled us to stumble on a scheme that enabled key workers to receive assistance from the Government towards getting their own homes.

Needless to say, that we pursued this option and by the help of God with prudence, planning and determination, that dream was realised. God's wisdom as found in the scriptures is always your best guide whenever you have options to consider. From the words of God, you will gain a fresh perspective that will make you think outside the box and birth in you great visions of victory ahead in your endeavours. God's word is a reservoir of fresh insight that multiplies your capability to outperform your contemporaries so that all the time, you are on the cutting edge of innovative inspiration to solve tomorrow's problems today, this ability will set you apart from the rest all the time.

20 Wisdom calls aloud outside; She raises her voice in the open squares. 21 She cries out in the chief concourses, At the openings of the gates in the city She speaks her words: 22 "How long, you simple ones, will you love simplicity? For scorners delight in their scorning, and fools hate knowledge 23 Turn at my rebuke; Surely, I will pour out my spirit on you; I will make my words known to you. **Proverbs 1:20-23**

If the axe is dull, and one does not sharpen the edge, then he must use more strength; But wisdom brings success. **Ecclesiastes 10:10**

Do not cast away your confidence in God because of a few temporary challenges you might have to face in the pursuit of your set vision in life, keep hold of your faith all the way. Let your focus rest squarely on the author and the finisher of your destiny outcomes in life. irrespective of who they might be in society or their experiences, don't let the ideas, values, words of discouragement, negative actions of those around you or their incorrect philosophies throw you off the course of faith in your God who has proved faithful to you time and time again in the past.

And Saul said to David, "You are not able to go against this Philistine to fight with him; for you are a youth, and he is a man of war from his youth." **1 Samuel 17:33**

With the help of God, you will keep on moving your mountains against all odds and despite all the obstacles on your route to success. You are ordained in God to break through all barriers of limitations in your life, however in your dealings with the issues of life, please ensure that you do not hold anyone who might have hurt you in the past in your mind. Living a life free of hurt and lavish forgiveness is essential to a life of constant victory.

22 So Jesus answered and said to them, "Have faith in God. 23 For assuredly, I say to you, whoever says to this mountain, 'Be removed and be cast into the sea,' and does not doubt in his heart, but believes that those things he says will be done, he will have whatever he says. 24 Therefore I say to you, whatever things you ask when you pray, believe that you receive them, and you will have them. 25 "And whenever you stand praying, if you have anything against anyone, forgive him, that your Father in heaven may also forgive you your trespasses. 26 But if you do not forgive, neither will your Father in heaven forgive your trespasses." **Mark 11:22-26**

Overcome every satanically inspired lying visions presented before you by the realisation of the prevailing sacrifice of God over your life and your past testimonials of God's unfailing love for you. Like David, remember all the victories that the Lord has given you in the past when you were in a tight corner, these would inspire fresh hope and belief in the ability of the unlimited God to deliver you once again.

11 And they overcame him by the blood of the Lamb and by the word of their testimony, and they did not love their lives to the death. **Revelation 12:11**

There are the fiery darts of doubt thrown at you every time to make you second guess your actions and water down your faith in your ever powerful God. Protect your heart from spiritual injury by using the shield of faith in God as described in **Ephesians 6:16**.

Remember in the power and resources of the Almighty God, you are totally unlimited in every dimension, if you keep this vision in your heart, everything becomes possible with God's help.

13 I can do all things through Christ who strengthens me. **Philippians 4:13**

23 Jesus said to him, "If you can believe, all things are possible to him who believes." **Mark 9:23**

David shut down the negative visions propagated by the enemy even though it was propagated by one of the highest authorities in his time. This gives us a vital lesson as we go through life. Learn to shut out anything that will steal away your confidence in God's words, everything will conform to the everlasting all powerful potent words of God who is alive forevermore.

34 But David said to Saul, "Your servant used to keep his father's sheep, and when a lion or a bear came and took a lamb out of the flock, 35 I went out after it and struck it, and delivered the lamb from its mouth; and when it arose against me, I caught it by its beard, and struck and killed it. 36 Your servant has killed both lion and bear; and this uncircumcised Philistine will be like one of them, seeing he has defied the armies of the living God." 37 Moreover David said, "The Lord, who delivered me from the paw of the lion and from the paw of the bear, He will deliver me from the hand of this Philistine." And Saul said to David, "Go, and the Lord be with you!" **1 Samuel 17:34-37.**

Conclusion
Keep your eyes firmly on God always to avoid the shame that will come to you when you allow yourself to be distracted from your God given vision for your journey in life. Unending victory and consistent success are for those who remain strong in their faith in the Almighty God. Heavens will commit divine supernatural resources into your life situations to keep giving you spectacular great outcomes that will always bring great honour and glory to God in every way.

32 Those who do wickedly against the covenant he shall corrupt with flattery; but the people who know their God shall be strong and carry out great exploits. **Daniel 11:32**

5 They looked to Him and were radiant, and their faces were not ashamed. 6 This poor man cried out, and the Lord heard him, and saved him out of all his troubles. 7 The angel of the Lord encamps all around those who fear Him And delivers them. **Psalm 34:5-7**

Pursue visions that are rooted in honour and reverence for God in all ways. It is time to shine for God in all areas of your life. Keep your eyes on Jesus, in Him you will find a way forward. If you do not know Jesus, you can come into a relationship today by asking Jesus sincerely to come into your heart right now.

A new door will open to you, you will obtain fresh visions of what you can do with your life that will bring glory to God and positively impact lives around you. Nobody is beyond God's redemption and no life is beyond is damaged by experiences of this life that can't be mended by God. All God asks from you is to take the first step towards Him right now. Acknowledge that God is near you and willing to give you a new lease of life if you give Him room in your heart. Remember these wise words from your maker and decide to be guided by Him always.

"The fear of the Lord is the beginning of wisdom, And the knowledge of the Holy One is understanding. **Proverbs 9:10**.

THE SEVENTH TIME
1 Kings 18:41-47

Mankind by nature is endowed with leadership and problem-solving capabilities that make us take initiative to exercise dominion as our vision becomes clear over a period on a matter. In our life's journey, the most uncomfortable time for us as a people is the time, we spend waiting for the manifestation of a vision yet, this is the most crucial time because every vision has a time appointed for it to manifest in full. The Almighty God will make everything fall in place perfectly together at His own appointed time frame which sometimes could be entirely different from our because God's time is comprehensively driven by the bigger picture of eternity as opposed to our parochial shortsighted pursuits which have limited impact in life.

For the vision is yet for an appointed time; But at the end it will speak, and it will not lie. Though it tarries, wait for it; Because it will surely come, It will not tarry. **Habakkuk 2:3**

11 He has made everything beautiful in its time. Also, He has put eternity in their hearts, except that no one can find out the work that God does from beginning to end. **Ecclesiastes 3:11**

Make the time to be intimate with God in the place of fellowship with the Holy Spirit to receive a vision from above to guide your next steps, what God reveals to you will be mysteries that in turn will produce a motivating drive in you to go faster and further than your peers.

But there is a spirit in man, And the breath of the Almighty gives him understanding. **Job 32:8**

11 Moreover the word of the Lord came to me, saying, "Jeremiah, what do you see?" And I said, "I see a branch of an almond tree." 12 Then the Lord said to me, "You have seen well, for I am ready to perform My word." **Jeremiah 1:11-12**

I will stand my watch and set myself on the rampart and watch to see what He will say to me, and what I will answer when I am corrected. 2 Then the Lord answered me and said: "Write the vision and make it plain on tablets, that he may run who reads it. **Habakkuk 2:1-2**

The things you both hear and see in the secret pavilion of God must birth a vision that will drive you and determine your actions in prayer. It propels you to keep praying until you get an answer from the Almighty God who always answers prayers.

41 Then Elijah said to Ahab, "Go up, eat and drink; for there is the sound of abundance of rain." 42 So Ahab went up to eat and drink. And Elijah went up to the top of Carmel; then he bowed down on the ground, and put his face between his knees, **1 Kings 18:41-42**.

Ultimate 'truth' is established by the confirmation of a vision as it manifests, every eye will see it because it is a totally 'new thing' different from everything you had seen, hoped for, or experienced so far. You will see the new thing God has for you if you keep looking for it intently. If you do not look, you might not see what God's Spirit is revealing to you, keep looking.

13 I would have lost heart, unless I had believed, In the land of the living. 14 Wait on the Lord; Be of good courage, And He shall strengthen your heart; Wait, I say, on the Lord! **Psalm 27:13-14**

12 For this reason I also suffer these things; nevertheless, I am not ashamed, for I know whom I have believed and am persuaded that

*He is able to keep what I have committed to Him until that Day.***2 Timothy 1:12**

Pursue your vision!
The vision you can see in the secret place of intimate fellowship with the trinity will drive you to put in the effort required to see its manifestation. You have a responsibility to pray your vision through to guarantee a breakthrough. To ensure this happens without delay, you must take on board the following principles as your way of life.

Do not compare yourself with others. Your journey and destiny assignments at each point in life is different from that of anyone else, even those so close to you. There is a specific race assigned to you to pursue, you must not abandon this race for any other thing even if all others are pursuing this!
Get rid of the distractions that can attract you away from your divine purpose, keep your eyes fixed on your author and finisher to always align to His path of life outlined for you. As your author, God is always writing a custom-made script for your journey of life, stick to the script He has written out for you, that is the race **you must run!**

Therefore, we also, since we are surrounded by so great a cloud of witnesses, let us lay aside every weight, and the sin which so easily ensnares us, and let us run with endurance the race that is set before us, **Hebrews 12:1**

Recognise your next phase and step into it. King Ahab's next assignment was to eat and drink as a signal of the end of a famine season as he the leader of the nation prepared himself for a new phase of restoration of the planting cycle. However, for Prophet Elijah, his next phase was to intensify prayers to prevail over all the opposing powers that wanted to contend against the manifestation of his prophetic utterance. To bring into existence the vision of greatness you have caught a hold of in the spirit realm in the natural world, you must not relent in prayers, never give up rather pursue the manifestation in the place of praying desperately as one who has no other option but God's intervention. This might mean you have to go again and again even up to seven times.

1 For Zion's sake I will not hold My peace, and for Jerusalem's sake I will not rest, until her righteousness goes forth as brightness, and her salvation as a lamp that burns. 2 The Gentiles shall see your righteousness, And all kings your glory. You shall be called by a new name, Which the mouth of the Lord will name. 3 You shall also be a crown of glory in the hand of the Lord, And a royal diadem in the hand of your God. 4 You shall no longer be termed Forsaken, nor shall your land any more be termed Desolate; But you shall be called Hephzibah, and your land Beulah; For the Lord delights in you, and your land shall be married. 5 For as a young man marries a virgin So shall your sons marry you; And as the bridegroom rejoices over the bride, so shall your God rejoice over you. 6 I have set watchmen on your walls, O Jerusalem; They shall never hold their Peace Day or night. You who make mention of the Lord, do not keep silent, 7 And give Him no rest till He establishes And till He makes Jerusalem a praise in the earth. **Isaiah 62:1-7**

See the vision and determine to do all to accomplish it. Jesus saw the future afar off and took time to pray for their manifestation for all in John chapter seventeen. Catch a vision of those to whom you have submitted to by imbibing their spirit through determined disciplined followership **2 Kings 2:1-15**.

Commitment to serve means you will be blessed as you receive those who come in the name of the Lord, you will not miss your own reward for sacrificial service. Keep looking until you see what they see in the spirit even if you must keep checking again and again 'seven times' like the servant of Elijah the prophet who had seen the vision in the spirit realm had to.
You are yet to see the glorious next phase of your life that God has pre-packed and made ready for you, it will blow your mind and launch you into another level of global glory.
However, you might have to go again and again in faith filled prayer fellowship with the Highest God for it to be manifest.

Do not come down or abandon your vision because those around you cannot see what you are seeing in your future, hold on firmly to the vision, it will surely come to pass even if there is a delay, you can be rest assured, God will never fail or disappoint your faith in Him.

For the vision is yet for an appointed time; But at the end it will speak, and it will not lie. Though it tarries, wait for it; Because it will surely come, It will not tarry. **Habakkuk 2:3**

My story of getting my dream career

Write the vision you see and let your heart be impregnated with that vision as you focus on the revelation you caught in the spirit. Many years ago, I came into the country with a passion for teaching which was my innate skill set from my home country. Everyone I met in the southeast part of the country to where I arrived counselled me to go for a security role since this was popular and very easy to get into because it involved a few days of training, and the pay then was good.

I considered and evaluated this against my passion and knew this was just not for me. As is my practice, I committed all things to God and asked that His will for my life be done. I made the necessary plans to get the relevant National Insurance number documents to allow me to work and get into the 'system' whilst making applications to the job centre. A neighbour of my brother who was in the security field took my details and offered to connect me with the security company where he worked. Amazingly, despite this very personal connection, nothing came of it, God shut that door.

The door the Lord opened to me for my first permanent job was that of a parking attendant in the borough of Westminster which was one of the most expensive for parking in London. I did this for about a year making the most of a very challenging season in my life. To get by, I had to do very long hours of constant patrolling of the streets to enforce the traffic parking regulations. It was not a popular or particularly easy role. We were hated by the residents, despised by the drivers, and reviled by the people on the streets who saw us as scavengers who picked on people to get money out of them. Some were under the impression that we had a quota of tickets we must deliver daily to earn our keep and to make matters worse, there were quite a few bad eggs among the civil enforcement team (the posh name for 'parking attendants') who let the profession down.

In those days, God helped me to have a positive mental attitude to the work converting the patrols to a time to prayer walk the streets of Westminster while carrying out my duties diligently without cutting corners as some of my colleagues were doing. In my time on the street, because of constant patrolling, I wore out three pairs of strong patrol footwear. I always carried along with me my pocket bible that I engaged with studiously whenever I had a break from my duties. Every opportunity on the street was used to be a model believer doing good to all people I met as much as was within my powers to use my discretion when enforcing the parking regulations.

Over time, I received the favour of God and the favour of men as I did my duty with a humane face, this opened doors to me, and I began to really enjoy the role even though it was tiring. However, despite the seeming success, favour, and joy I derived from being on the street in all weathers being a help to all I met, I kept my dream of going back into teaching.

One day, while on my lunch break, I came across an advert by the Bromley Collegiate which was made up of seven schools who clubbed together to offer those who might want to train as teachers in secondary schools an opportunity to come for an open day at one of their schools at Orpington. This was a place I had never been to before but just had an idea that once you get to Lewisham bus station you will find vehicles going to Orpington. The open day was on a Saturday following a night vigil in my local church on Friday which would close in the wee hours of the morning. Bearing in mind that I had patrolled all day on Friday, and I had to return home and then attend the vigil with my family going on public transport from our accommodation in Shooters Hill then, it was a very strong temptation to let that day pass.

God honoured my yearning to get back into teaching by supernaturally strengthening me through the day's work and vigil of Friday into the early hours of Saturday. I got home, slept for a few hours, and woke up strong, refreshed as one who had slept for ten hours. I found my way to the open day and actively engaged with enthusiasm with the event. By the time the event ended, I got an invitation to come for an interview as a potential candidate for the role of unqualified teacher who would be trained by the Bromley Collegiate while I work in the school teaching science. Suffice to say that by God's grace my dream of returning to teaching in the United Kingdom came to pass, I obtained my Qualified Teacher Status (QTS) completed my Newly Qualified Teacher (NQT) phase and went on to teach for more than a decade in what was a very rewarding career. Write your vision clearly, make it plain and run with it even if you must go the seventh time, it will be worth it in the end when you win. Your future is bright!

HOW WILL YOU GO?
2 Kings 2:1

Wisdom is the correct application of knowledge or information you have access to, it shapes your approach to life and the use of your limited time on this earth relative to eternity. We do not have a continuous unending existence here on earth, heaven is our permanent abode if you are a believer in the Lord Jesus and have accepted His gift of salvation purchased for you on the cross of Calvary. While here on earth making our way to eternity with God in His kingdom, be careful how you live, make the very best use of every time you have.

So, teach us to number our days, so that we may gain a heart of wisdom. **Psalm 90:12**

See then that you walk circumspectly, not as fools but as wise,**Ephesians 5:15.**

God will welcome unto Himself in the appointed time those who while here on earth were intimate with God in their unique fellowship of faith with Him. Some examples of those who have gone ahead of us are recorded in scriptures are — Enoch walked with God so perfectly that God took him unto Himself in heaven without allowing him to experience death. This was effectively the first experience of being caught up to heaven in a 'rapture like experience' in the Old Testament times.

And Enoch walked with God; and he was not, for God took him
Genesis 5:24

Elisha walked with God passionately by pursuing Him in his unwavering service to his earthly master's ministry -the prophet Elijah. The Almighty God rewarded Elisha with a double portion of the anointing on his master Elijah.

1 And it came to pass, when the Lord was about to take up Elijah into heaven by a whirlwind, that Elijah went with Elisha from Gilgal. 2 Then Elijah said to Elisha, "Stay here, please, for the Lord has sent me on to Bethel." But Elisha said, "As the Lord lives, and as your soul lives, I will not leave you!" So, they went down to Bethel. 3 Now the sons of the prophets who were at Bethel came out to Elisha, and said to him, "Do you know that the Lord will take away your master from over you today?" And he said, "Yes, I know; keep silent!" 4 Then Elijah said to him, "Elisha, stay here, please, for the Lord has sent me on to Jericho." But he said, "As the Lord lives, and as your soul lives, I will not leave you!" So, they came to Jericho. 5 Now the sons of the prophets who were at Jericho came to Elisha and said to him, "Do you know that the Lord will take away your master from over you today?" So, he answered, "Yes, I know; keep silent!" 6 Then Elijah said to him, "Stay here, please, for the Lord has sent me on to Jordan." But he said, "As the Lord lives, and as your soul lives, I will not leave you!" So, the two of them went on. 7 And fifty men of the sons of the prophets went and stood facing them at a distance, while the two of them stood by the Jordan. 8 Now Elijah took his mantle, rolled it up, and struck the water; and it was divided this way and that, so that the two of them crossed over on dry ground. 9 And so it was, when they had crossed over, that Elijah said to Elisha, "Ask! What may I do for you, before I am taken away from you?" Elisha said, "Please let a double portion of your spirit be upon me." 10 So he said, "You have asked a hard thing. Nevertheless, if you see me when I am taken from you, it shall be so for you; but if not, it shall not be so." 11 Then it happened, as they continued and talked, that suddenly a chariot of fire appeared with horses of fire and separated the two of them; and Elijah went up by a whirlwind into heaven. 12 And Elisha saw it, and he cried out, "My *father, my father, the chariot of Israel and its horsemen!" So, he saw him no more. And he took hold of his own clothes and tore them into two pieces. **13** He also took up the mantle of Elijah that had fallen from him and went back and stood by the bank of the Jordan. **14** Then he took the mantle of Elijah that had fallen from him, and struck the water, and said, "Where is the Lord God of Elijah?" And when he also had struck the water, it was divided this way and that; and Elisha crossed over. **15** Now when the sons of the prophets who were from Jericho saw him, they said, "The spirit of Elijah rests on Elisha." And they came to meet him and bowed to the ground before him.* **2 Kings 2:1-15**

What will you be remembered for in your service to the Almighty God where He has placed you today? Would you have a similar testimony of dogged faithfulness, or will you be remembered as the one who dropped off the race?

Hebrews 11:1-38 - contains the stories of the great heroes of faith of old who walked with God in their time and did exponential exploits to pave the way for us to have faith.

Jesus, our perfect example, showed us how-to walk-in God's principles despite various contradictions of the culture and society in His days. Jesus completed His mandate on earth, likewise you must work during the day to finish strong in your faith so you could attain to every potential in Christ. On the cross of calvary, He declared, 'it is finished'.

30 So when Jesus had received the sour wine, He said, "It is finished!" And bowing His head, He gave up His spirit. **John 19:30**

Nobody except God knows the time He has set for your life or for His return to this world at the rapture of the saints of God. We must all be ready by keeping a focused heart on the vision of eternity with God rather than losing sight of His return as faithful stewards of divine grace.

51 Behold, I tell you a mystery: We shall not all sleep, but we shall all be changed— 52 in a moment, in the twinkling of an eye, at the last trumpet. For the trumpet will sound, and the dead will be raised incorruptible, and we shall be changed. **1 Corinthians 15:51-52**

45 "Who then is a faithful and wise servant, whom his master made ruler over his household, to give them food in due season? 46 Blessed is that servant whom his master, when he comes, will find so doing. 47 Assuredly, I say to you that he will make him ruler over all his goods. 48 But if that evil servant says in his heart, 'My master is delaying his coming,' 49 and begins to beat his fellow servants, and to eat and drink with the drunkards, 50 the master of that servant will come on a day when he is not looking for him and at an hour that he is not aware of, 51 and will cut him in two and appoint him his portion with the hypocrites. There shall be weeping and gnashing of teeth. **Matthew 24:45-51**.

Conclusion

Will you be ready when the Lord calls you to your heavenly home? No unclean thing will go through to that place no matter how acceptable or culturally popular it is here on earth.

27 But there shall by no means enter it anything that defiles, or causes an abomination or a lie, but only those who are written in the Lamb's Book of Life. **Revelation 21:27**

If this is your hope, you must purge yourself of all that can corrupt or disqualify you now when you still can do so.

2 Beloved, now we are children of God; and it has not yet been revealed what we shall be, but we know that when He is revealed, we shall be like Him, for we shall see Him as He is. 3 And everyone who has this hope in Him purifies himself, just as He is pure. **1 John 3:2-3**

Friend, is your name written in the book of life? Have you made a conscious choice to make Jesus the Lord of your life? Do you still follow Him, or have you become distracted? Come to the foot of the Cross now.

SOARING ON EAGLES WINGS
Daniel 6:1-3

T here are many types of motion which thrives by converting potential energy to kinetic energy. The more kinetic energy you have the greater your speed of motion which creates movement. It is possible to cover a distance in various ways such as crawling, walking, jogging, sprinting, leaping, flying, or soaring. In all these instances, it is essential that there is enough Kinetic energy generated to overcome the natural enemy of motion which is called inertia. Just as it is in the physical sciences, so it is in the spiritual realm.

Technically your motion in the spiritual realm of accomplishment could be either a crawl, walk, jog, run, leap, sprint or soaring above all obstacles of spiritual relevance and growth into your ordained purpose in life. The story of a fellow believer who lived in the very dark days of the Kingdom of Babylon that was heavily steeped in idolatry and ungodliness is a useful guide to us in our world today. The vision Daniel had at the beginning of his stay in Babylon kept him soaring in faith above all others in his days. If we learn from the example of Daniel, each one of us will also experience his awesome success in living out his faith in a dark and depraved world where we find ourselves today.

King Darius decided on the future progress of his kingdom.

The quality of your thinking is driven by the overall vision you have in your heart, this in turn will determine the heights you will soar to in life.

*For as he thinks in his heart, so is he. "Eat and drink!" he says to you, But his heart is not with you.***Proverbs 23:7**

The great vision you have must dominate every though you permit into your heart, let these be what things are good, have virtue, are honourable and greater than whatever you have or are experiencing right now.

*⁶ Be anxious for nothing, but in everything by prayer and supplication, with thanksgiving, let your requests be made known to God; ⁷ and the peace of God, which surpasses all understanding, will guard your hearts and minds through Christ Jesus. ⁸ Finally, brethren, whatever things are true, whatever things are noble, whatever things are just, whatever things are pure, whatever things are lovely, whatever things are of good report, if there is any virtue and if there is anything praiseworthy—meditate on these things.***Philippians 4:6-8**

Saturate your mind with great dreams always if you want to always be many steps above others soaring high in your ordained destiny. Adopt the habit of always being persuaded of better things about others irrespective of their backgrounds, see the good potential in them inspire of their current flaws.

But, beloved, we are confident of better things concerning you, yes, things that accompany salvation, though we speak in this manner. **Hebrews 6:9**

Norman Vincent Peale wrote about positive thinking in his many books in his lifetime, but the Almighty God wrote the Holy Bible for us which contains possibility thinking, let your mind and thoughts be renewed with great fresh visions inspired by the verses of scriptures all the time. The individual who will soar on Eagles wings must constantly add value by investing in the development of others around them through active facilitation of platforms for them to perform even if they must learn on the job making mistakes along the way. You can't be great alone all by yourself, you need others around you, the vision that will keep you soaring above your contemporaries is a lot greater than what you can accomplish all on your own.

*⁹ Two are better than one, because they have a good reward for their labour. ¹⁰ For if they fall, one will lift his companion. But woe to him who is alone when he falls, for he has no one to help him up.***Ecclesiastes 4:9-10**.

The concept of TEAMS is to Multiply output and performance. Each one of us in union with God at work in our individual lives alongside those that God places in our lives will fulfil the dreams we have. Your vision must not just see the great future but also scan around to see those who will help you fulfil it. This is the reason the Lord created mankind to be a social being and encourages believers to optimise their joint faith in God to produce multiplied results all the time. You can't really soar to greater heights if you are a loner or a one person ban who never interacts or works with others, at best your progress will be visible however it will be a lot less than it could be if you had worked with those of the same vision as you God had strategically placed around you. Remember, it is not the people God brings to you but God working in and through them to help you keep soaring, this is the secret of unending achievement in any area of endeavour.

*How could one chase a thousand, and two put ten thousand to flight, unless their Rock had sold them, and the Lord had surrendered them?***Deuteronomy 32:30**.

*¹⁹ "Again I say to you that if two of you agree on earth concerning anything that they ask, it will be done for them by My Father in heaven.***Matthew 18:19**.

The King was already born great through his heritage and antecedent but, driven by his great vision, he wanted to be greater still! Those who will soar always want to be more and more fruitful in all their ways. Do not be satisfied with the progress you have made so far, be your own honest ruthless harsh critic of yourself, find ways you could do better next time so that you are ever improving, ever advancing.

*⁸ By this My Father is glorified, that you bear much fruit; so, you will be My disciples.***John 15:8.**

Just like King Darius**,** take time to strategically optimise the opportunities and resources you have driven by the realisation that you will not live forever therefore, they take every time they must build a glorious legacy. Make the most of every opportunity that comes your way, time is running out for you to complete the mandate of God upon you in every area of your life. Those who soar are always in a race against time to achieve the best for their lives as a matter of principle, they allocate specific tasks to time rather than waste it aimlessly.

So, teach us to number our days, that we may gain a heart of wisdom. **Psalm 90:12**.

Remain irrevocably on a mission of always fruitfulness and keep on abounding in the work of their hands or mandate. King Darius wanted more fruit from the resources of his Kingdom and looked for those who would bring more value and profit to him. Likewise, God desires more fruitfulness from us all the time not less, if we are imitating God in exercising the mandate of dominion on the earth, to keep pursuing the vision of soaring high, we cannot demand any less of ourselves!

¹⁶ You did not choose Me, but I chose you and appointed you that you should go and bear fruit, and that your fruit should remain, that whatever you ask the Father in My name He may give you. **John 15:16**.

⁵⁸ Therefore, my beloved brethren, be steadfast, immovable, always abounding in the work of the Lord, knowing that your labour is not in vain in the Lord. **1 Corinthians 15:58**

Conclusion

The Spirit of excellence driven by your vision will make you stand out from the crowd irrespective of your background, ethnicity or start in life. This comes from the Holy Spirit and will make you shine the brightest among the crowd of others. There is still much more to come in your life and future, keep burning brighter like the sun, consume on the altar of greatness laziness, dealing with a slack hand and all forms of complacency, there is more ahead of you than all you have enjoyed so far. Get ready to shine even brighter than before.

[41] *There is one glory of the sun, another glory of the moon, and another glory of the stars; for one star differs from another star in glory.* **1 Corinthians 15:41.**

THE SPIRIT OF EXCELLENCE AND PREFERENCE
Daniel 6:3

T here are many ways to define what excellence is, in a

nutshell, it is to do your task so well that there is no need to review, revise, redo, upgrade, revisit, improve upon what has been done or to re-evaluate your work to see further areas of improvements. To be excellent is to be perfect just like God is perfect in all His ways and in all He always does.

48 Therefore you shall be perfect, just as your Father in heaven is perfect. **Matthew 5:48**.

There is no one who is naturally capable of being excellent because of the wretched human nature often called our flesh that will always want to get in the way as described by the Apostle Paul.

13 Has then what is good become death to me? Certainly not! But sin, that it might appear sin, was producing death in me through what is good, so that sin through the commandment might become exceedingly sinful. 14 For we know that the law is spiritual, but I am carnal, sold under sin. 15 For what I am doing, I do not understand. For what I will to do, that I do not practice; but what I hate, that I do. 16 If then, I do what I will not to do, I agree with the law that it is good. 17 But now, it is no longer I who do it, but sin that dwells in me. 18 For I know that in me (that is, in my flesh) nothing good dwells; for to will is present with me, but how to perform what is good I do not find. ¹⁹ For the good that I will to do, I do not do; but the evil I will not to do, that I practice. ²⁰ Now if I do what I will not to do, it is no longer I who do it, but sin that dwells in me. ²¹ I find then a law, that evil is present with me, the one who wills to do good. ²² For I delight in the law of God according to the inward man. ²³ But I see another law in my members, warring against the law of my mind, and bringing me into captivity to the law of sin which is in my members. ²⁴ O wretched man that I am! Who will deliver me from this body of death? ²⁵ I thank God—through Jesus Christ our Lord! So then, with the mind I serve the law of God, but with the flesh the law of sin. **Romans 7: 13-25**

The potential to become excellent and perfect comes to you when you become transformed in your human nature through the experience of salvation in Christ Jesus. Following the salvation experience, you are then new creatures renewed in the thinking of your mind by holy scriptures found in the bible. Divine power is released to you to live as God's child and override the flesh's desires as God's Holy Spirit works through us when we believe in Jesus and accept Him into our lives. From that moment, we are given the power to be a child of God. All condemnation from our horrible past is forgiven so that the devil can no longer hold us to ransom because of the sinfulness of the past.

There is therefore now no condemnation to those who are in Christ Jesus, who do not walk according to the flesh, but according to the Spirit. ² For the law of the Spirit of life in Christ Jesus has made me free from the law of sin and death. ³ For what the law could not do in that it was weak through the flesh, God did by sending His own Son in the likeness of sinful flesh, on account of sin: He condemned sin in the flesh, ⁴ that the righteous requirement of the law might be fulfilled in us who do not walk according to the flesh but according to the Spirit. ⁵ For those who live according to the flesh set their minds on the things of the flesh, but those who live according to the Spirit, the things of the Spirit. ⁶ For to be carnally minded is death, but to be spiritually minded is life and peace. ⁷ Because the carnal mind is enmity against God; for it is not subject to the law of God, nor indeed can be. *⁸ So then, those who are in the flesh cannot please God.***Romans 8:1-8**.

Our spiritual encounter at rebirth in Christ brings us out of the obscurity of sinfulness we had been conformed to into a marvellous new light in God, our thoughts are refined and become excellent in Christ. A new glory will overshadow all areas of your life as you continue forward in Christ.

⁸ Then your light shall break forth like the morning, your healing shall spring forth speedily, and your righteousness shall go before you; The glory of the Lord shall be your rear guard. **Isaiah 58:8**

The spirit of excellence is a gift from God we obtain because He graciously releases this to us from above as part of the gifts and benefits of salvation in Christ. As it originates from God, it is superior to any other source of excellence or wisdom in the Earth even if these are great philosophers or literary giants of our time, God's wisdom from above is superior to every wisdom found on the earth through all the generations simply because God is the source of all wisdom.

²⁷ John answered and said, "A man can receive nothing unless it has been given to him from heaven. **John 3:27**

*³¹ He who comes from above is above all; he who is of the earth is earthly and speaks of the earth. He who comes from heaven is above all.***John 3:31**

Ultimately, vision and the spirit of excellence births distinction in you and can make you ten times better than your nearest contemporary. The unsearchable wisdom of God that sustains creation will work in you through the Holy Spirit who now abides in you at rebirth to give to you on a regular basis ideas unseen or unheard that will always trump over those around you from others.

¹⁷ As for these four young men, God gave them knowledge and skill in all literature and wisdom; and Daniel had understanding in all visions and dreams. ¹⁸ Now at the end of the days, when the king had *said that they should be brought in, the chief of the eunuchs brought them in before Nebuchadnezzar. ¹⁹ Then the king interviewed them, and among them all none was found like Daniel, Hananiah, Mishael, and Azariah; therefore, they served before the king. ²⁰ And in all matters of wisdom and understanding about which the king examined them, he found them ten times better than all the magicians and astrologers who were in all his realm.***Daniel 1:17-20**.

However even among those who are excellent and distinct, you can still go higher by growing in excellence just as Daniel did while in Babylon as an immigrant slave who rose through the ranks to become the foremost civil servant in the employment of the King. Let it be your unwavering vision to always be distinguished in excellence among the excellent anywhere you are, do not settle for anything less than excellence in all you do if you want to be the preferred one always.

²¹ Thus Daniel continued until the first year of King Cyrus. **Daniel 1:21**

<u>This Daniel kept on growing</u> in grace, in his area of gifting, in mission, passion, assignment and distinction above his excellent colleagues, what was his secret?

Consistent vision of Diligence in all he did in the Kingdom of Babylon made him qualified to stand to offer counsel to the King and the royal court even though he was a foreigner, he knew more than most of the indigenes simply because he gave himself to study and research. How are you performing in the place where you are today? Are you diligent or are you sadly a very poor example of excellence because of your non- callant attitude to pursuit of excellence because you are lacking a clear vision? This quality kept him ever relevant in the service of the king, it gave him an opportunity to display the multitude of treasures of wisdom in him.

But we have this treasure in earthen vessels, that the excellence of the power may be of God and not of us **2 Corinthians 4:7**.

If it worked for Daniel in an ungodly secular regime, it would work for you too wherever you are today.

Daniel had a vibrant spiritual relationship with Jehovah God, the King of all kings. This meant that he did not just stand before the king of Babylon but stood consistently in prayer before the Almighty God just like Elijah did.

And Elijah the Tishbite, of the inhabitants of Gilead, said to Ahab, "As the Lord God of Israel lives, before whom I stand, there shall not be dew nor rain these years, except at my word." **1 Kings 17:1**

To qualify to stand before God, out of a vision to be distinct and accepted before e the presence of God, he lived a life of purity and holiness before God who cannot behold sinfulness.

Behold what manner of love the Father has bestowed on us, that we should be called children of God! Therefore, the world does not know us, because it did not know Him. ² Beloved, now we are children of God; and it has not yet been revealed what we shall be, but we know that when He is revealed, we shall be like Him, for we shall see Him as He is. ³ And everyone who has this hope in Him purifies himself, just as He is pure. **1 John 3:1-3**

If you want the Lord to use, you in your generation then you must purge yourself of all evil and be reserved for God's use in every place you find yourself This made Daniel a man of integrity in all his affairs in the Kingdom.

Like Daniel, you must develop and maintain a vibrant prayer life notwithstanding how occupied or busy you might be, let communion with God be a top priority in your day, this is your lifeline and constant connection to the flow of the divine supernatural into every area of your life. Never let the vision of prayer communion with the most-high God die in your life because you are now full of responsibility, it must be your own personal priority for you to remain an evergreen innovative leader of your time who will be remember for outstanding distinction long after you are gone.

⁴ So the governors and satraps sought to find some charge against Daniel concerning the kingdom; but they couldfind no charge or fault, because he was faithful; nor was there any error or fault found in him. ⁵ Then these men said, "We shall not find any charge against this Daniel unless we find it against him concerning the law of his God." ⁶ So these governors and satraps thronged before the king, and said thus to him: "King Darius, live forever! ⁷ All the governors of the kingdom, the administrators and satraps, the counsellors and advisors, have consulted together to establish a royal statute and to make a firm decree, that whoever petitions any god or man for thirty days, except you, O king, shall be cast into the den of lions. ⁸ Now, O king, establish the decree and sign the writing, so that it cannot be changed, according to the law of the Medes and Persians, which does not alter." ⁹ Therefore King Darius signed the written decree. ¹⁰ Now when Daniel knew that the writing was signed, he went home. And in his upper room, with his windows open toward Jerusalem, he knelt down on his knees three times that day, and prayed and gave thanks before his God, as was his custom since early days. **Daniel 6:4-10.**

Do not let prayer slip through the cracks of your day, schedule it, put it in the dairy as well as on your to-do list every day, be consistent and committed to it. The place of prayer is the place of the release of divine power and revelations to solve the myriad of issues in your day as well as tomorrows emerging problems today through the insight the Holy Spirit gives to you as you spend time in fellowship with Him in prayer and meditation on scriptures.

⁹ But as it is written: "Eye has not seen, nor ear heard, nor have entered into the heart of man The things which God has prepared for those who love Him." ¹⁰ But God has revealed them to us through His Spirit. For the Spirit searches all things, yes, the deep things of God. ¹¹ For what man knows the things of a man except the spirit of the man which is in him? Even so no one knows the things of God except the Spirit of God. ¹² Now we have received, not the spirit of the world, but the Spirit who is from God, that we might know the things that have been freely given to us by God. **1 Corinthians 2:9-12**

Regularly seeking the presence of the Lord in fasting was another secret of Daniel in Babylon, he was seeking God not gold in the kingdom service **Daniel 10:1-21**. How passionate are you about God's presence? How deep do you want to go daily with God?

One thing I have desired of the Lord, that will I seek: All the days of my life, To behold the beauty of the Lord, And to inquire in His temple. **Psalm 27:4**

As the deer pants for the water brooks, so pants my soul for You, O God. ² My soul thirsts for God, for the living God. When shall I come and appear before God? **Psalm 42:1-2**

There must be a personal hunger for more of God in your life affairs not less, this vision will keep driving you into His presence **Isaiah 55:1-3**.

Conclusion

What you are hungry for will be your priority wherever you are. There is fame, glory, honour, riches out there but these are all vanity and chasing of the wind **Ecclesiastes 2:1-26.** The presence of God is the real deal, seek for this with all your heart.

¹⁴ I will be found by you, says the Lord, and I will bring you back from your captivity; I will gather you from all the nations and from all the places where I have driven you, says the Lord, and I will bring you to the place from which I cause you to be carried away captive **Jeremiah 29:14**

If you have turned back from following God, return to the foot of the Cross again to seek Godly wisdom the principal thing you need to succeed in life.

RISE AND WALK!
Acts 3:1-10

'Arise and shine' in the context of the scripture in Isaiah 60:1 is a divine command to you as an individual. Since the Almighty God is just and faithful, He will not ask us to do what is beyond our capacity to do, on the contrary, He will challenge us to come out of our comfort zone which limits us and step out by faith into a new reality of what things can be in Christ Jesus. This kind of change starts from within us as a spiritual transaction that we engage with in God's presence that transcends into the realm of physical manifestations called miracles, signs, and wonders. You must have a paradigm shift in your thinking and expectations from your time in His divine presence, expect big, expect the impossible, expect the promises of God to come to pass, the Almighty God is near you to visit you comprehensively.

... if you shall say to this mountain...

23 For assuredly, I say to you, whoever says to this mountain, 'Be removed and be cast into the sea,' and does not doubt in his heart, but believes that those things he says will be done, he will have whatever he says. 24 Therefore I say to you, whatever things you ask when you pray, believe that you receive them, and you will have them. **Mark 11:23-24**

One of the features of the mountains that make them so formidable is their well-defined structures that have defied time, environmental change as well as seasons to become the defining features of a landscape. You cannot escape them because of their prominence and their ability to make all things including the ecosystems revolve around their existence. Mountains often become the reference point from which all things take their bearing. Similarly, long term or lifelong difficult issues in our lives can both confine us and define us.

The lame man had a lifelong problem that seems to have been ordained from heaven above, it defied all human interventions applied in all the body of science and medicine. It eventually confined this man to only one way of surviving as a career path and this was to beg for a living. The physical body handicap of this man who coincidentally had his name usurped by the description of his problem, rechristened him thus redefining him in society.

No one saw him in the light of his potential, ability or capability, his problems redefined him. Sadly, probably due to many failed attempts to break free from this mould the world cast upon him, this man too had resigned to 'fate' and came to accept his lot in life with at most a feeble hope of a better deal sometime, somewhere one day. This is a tragedy of a lifelong
problem we might be nursing but today the Almighty is saying to you emphatically, arise and shine, your light has come!

The mountain-like lifelong challenges in the life of this lame man limited his access to help and helpers, those who came around him perpetuated and reinforced the image of a helpless person to whom life had dealt with so badly that deserves mega pity. The type of help, words they spoke kept his experiences and expectations at this same level of helpless hopelessness with only one future pathway guaranteed, to beg for a living. The lame man needed both a new vision of greatness alongside a change of mindset and environmental stimulus. Irrespective of how low you might be right now; you still have potential for a great turnaround once the right indices of favourable conditions come your way.

"For there is hope for a tree, if it is cut down, that it will sprout again, and that its tender shoots will not cease. **Job 14:7**

These may be in form of the encouraging words bubbling up in your heart, the bright alternative future you can envision or imagine in your heart or indeed real present practical helper of destiny that God will place in your path at that crucial time you are in the valley of decision. Remain sensitive to the Holy Spirit and do not miss your time of change that is coming your way, keep watching and waiting for it, you will have a new story of glory to tell the whole world just like this man in our story did.

I returned and saw under the sun that— The race is not to the swift, nor the battle to the strong, nor bread to the wise, nor riches to men of understanding, nor favour to men of skill; But time and chance happen to them all. ¹² For man also does not know his time: Like fish taken in a cruel net, like birds caught in a snare, So the sons of men are snared in an evil time, when it falls suddenly upon them. **Ecclesiastes 9:11-12.**

What vision of the future you see with the eye of hope and faith in the hour of your greatest need is often the key to your breakthrough in the debilitating circumstances around you, this is why the scriptures recommend that no matter what you are facing right now, keep looking unto Jesus the author and finisher of your faith and fate in life. Expect good news, good opportunities, good solutions, good outcomes in every part of each day that the Almighty God sends your way, what you expect will manifest as your reality in fulfilment of the vision of your heart. This was the experience that Job had when he was going through some challenges of life.

For the thing I greatly feared has come upon me, and what I dreaded has happened to me. **Job 3:25.**

As soon as the lame man saw Peter and John cross his path on that fateful day, he put aside all the previous disappointing experiences he had had before this time and looked at them with optimism that this might just be the good break from a series of ugly encounters he had been hoping for. Armed with this attitude, he soared to a new altitude of maximizing the moment at hand, making the most of every opportunity that the Apostles were near to him. It is no wonder that Peter, a man under the influence of the Holy Spirit saw the hunger for a change of circumstances in the lame man and demanded his whole focus and attention at that time.

redeeming the time because the days are evil. **Ephesians 5:16**

'Look on us' the phrase Peter used to concentrate and arrest the attention of the lame man was designed to accomplish a couple of things in his life, these include provoking a fresh new vision of what life can be if you are not limited by the limits that had dogged your life for so long. The lame man was able to see and really see other people who were not physically challenged and with a mind unfettered by limitations imagine himself as one who could walk on his two feet.

Secondly, this phrase was designed to wean the lame man off 'human pity' whose origin and motives were often convoluted based on the hidden objectives of those who visited the temple. The charity which he had often received from many who treated him as a nameless temple appendage of convenience to their piety was mostly out of scorn for the inconvenience his presence constituted to their worship experience rather than genuine love of mercy.

This phrase was designed to challenge him to look higher, hope better and deeper for a once in a lifetime change that could come. God is saying the same words to you right now in your own situations, look on God and let your countenance be no longer sad just like Hannah did when she went into the presence of God to pour out her heart to God rather than man in the temple.

⁹ So Hannah arose after they had finished eating and drinking in Shiloh. Now Eli the priest was sitting on the seat by the doorpost of the tabernacle of the Lord. ¹⁰ And she was in bitterness of soul and prayed to the Lord and wept in anguish. ¹¹ Then she made a vow and said, "O Lord of hosts, if You will indeed look on the affliction of Your maidservant and remember me, and not forget Your maidservant, but will give Your maidservant a male child, then I will give him to the Lord all the days of his life, and no razor shall come upon his head." 12 And it happened, as she continued praying before the Lord, that Eli watched her mouth. 13 Now Hannah spoke in her heart; only her lips moved, but her voice was not heard. Therefore, Eli thought she was drunk. 14 So Eli said to her, "How long will you be drunk? Put your wine away from you!" 15 But Hannah answered and said, "No, my lord, I am a woman of sorrowful spirit. I have drunk neither wine nor intoxicating drink but have poured out my soul before the Lord. 16 Do not consider your maidservant a wicked woman, for out of the abundance of my complaint and grief I have spoken until now." 18 And she said, "Let your maidservant find favour in your sight." So, the woman went her way and ate, and her face was no longer sad. **1 Samuel 1:9-18**

These words propelled the lame man into the realm of daring hope for the miraculous visitation of God, may God's words to you birth a miracle in you right now in Jesus' name Amen.

Who will go for us is Heaven's daily cry, God is looking for the individual who will allow Him to flow through them in the miraculous power of manifestation. If you are saved and redeemed by faith in Christ Jesus, you qualify to carry God's power to your generation just like the Apostles did in their time. God's spirit in you is ready to flow to the overflowing now as He did then if only you have a vision of this happening through you.

37 On the last day, that great day of the feast, Jesus stood and cried out, saying, "If anyone thirsts, let him come to Me and drink. 38 He who believes in Me, as the Scripture has said, out of his heart will flow rivers of living water." 39 But this He spoke concerning the Spirit, whom those believing in Him would receive; for the Holy Spirit was not yet given, because Jesus was not yet glorified. **John 7:37-39**.

Transmit your faith in God into the life situations and circumstances of others you meet daily as active ambassadors of the true and living God, your world is waiting for your manifestation of divine glory.

Catch a fresh vision that will drive you to arise and shine for Jesus in your community with the glorious power of God. There is no partiality with God, if you pay the price the disciples of old paid, God too will use you in your generation right where you are.

19 For the earnest expectation of the creation eagerly waits for the revealing of the sons of God. 20 For the creation was subjected to futility, not willingly, but because of Him who subjected it in hope; 21 because the creation itself also will be delivered from the bondage of corruption into the glorious liberty of the children of God. **Romans 8:19-20**

These two disciples teach us bold active faith that makes you flow out in the compassion for the hurting around you without the protocols being observed. The disciples were desirous to see God work in the life of the downtrodden helpless man rather than tracking his background. True deep compassion is always the key to the release of the grace of God for the miraculous, therefore do not let the vision of true compassion for the suffering ever go dim.

12 Therefore, as the elect of God, holy and beloved, put-on tender mercies, kindness, humility, meekness, longsuffering; **Colossians 3:12**

Jesus demonstrated this at the feeding of the 5000, compassion was the key that burst open the dam of the miraculous provision to meet the pressing needs of the people notwithstanding their status on faith in God. Unless we go back to being passionate and compassionate for the people around us, there might not be divine miracles. This was the challenge of the early church believers and sadly is still the challenge of the church of God in our times.

4 Now the Passover, a feast of the Jews, was nearby. 5 Then Jesus lifted His eyes, and seeing a great multitude coming toward Him, He said to Philip, "Where shall we buy bread, that these may eat?" 6 But this He said to test him, for He Himself knew what He would do. 7 Philip answered Him, "Two hundred denarii worth of bread is not sufficient for them, that every one of them may have a little." 8 One of His disciples, Andrew, Simon Peter's brother, said to

Him, ⁹ "There is a lad here who has five barley loaves and two small fish, but what are they among so many?" ¹⁰ Then Jesus said, "Make the people sit down." Now there was much grass in the place. So the men sat down, in number about five thousand. ¹¹ And Jesus took the loaves, and when He had given thanks He distributed them ⁱ

a 1

to the disciples, and the disciples to those sitting down; and likewise of the fish, as much as they wanted. ¹² So when they were filled, He said to His disciples, "Gather up the fragments that remain, so that nothing is lost." ¹³ Therefore they gathered them up, and filled twelve baskets with the fragments of the five barley loaves which were left over by those who had eaten. **John 6: 4-13**

Let your light shine in this dark world, arise shine, your light has come, now is your time. When you have done your own part, the Almighty God does what He does best, the miraculous visitation of God takes place and there is joy and rejoicing as people see the miracles and offer praises to God who does miracles even in our times.

How long will you keep God waiting for you to step forward in His power? When will you catch this vision to arise and begin to harvest the ripe souls into God's Kingdom? The world is tired of sermons, teachings, theological debates, disagreements in His body, they are tired of being told they do not measure up to God's standards, this is not news to them, they know this.

The hurting world is looking for compassionate spirit driven believers who will take the power of God to meet them where they are at spiritually and draw them to Christ, remember except they see signs and wonders, they shall not believe **John 4:34-36.**

1

THE 'NOW ANOINTING'.
1 Samuel 10:1-7

T he book of Ecclesiastes 3:1 informs us that there is a right
time and a season for everything under the surface of the earth
ordained for all things including you, may you not miss your own
'now time' in Jesus' name Amen. This special 'now time of your life'
is programmed and orchestrated to release into your destiny divine
lifting, visitation, breakthrough as well as unending mercy, it is your
own set time of mercy Psalm 102:13. This is your time to pursue the
vision to arise and shine comprehensively, compellingly,
outstandingly, irresistibly, resounding, overwhelming, undisputed,
and impactfullY. **1 Corinthians 15:41**

Characteristics of this 'now anointing' include the following:
It is an ever-increasing grace fuelled by an ever-increasing faith in
God that enlarges your scope of glory as you feed your faith in God
on His words. It challenges you to have a new vision of what is not
apparent, but which has been promised us in scriptures.

[17] So then faith *comes* by hearing, and hearing by the word of God.

"Sing, O barren, you who have not borne! Break forth into singing,
and cry aloud, you who have not laboured with child! For
more are the children of the desolate Than the children of the
married woman," says the Lord. [2] *"Enlarge the place of your tent*

3

and let them stretch out the curtains of your dwellings; Do not spare; Lengthen your cords and strengthen your stakes. ³ For you shall expand to the right and to the left, and make the desolate cities inhabited. **Isaiah 54:1-3.**

This 'now anointing' is ever flourishing in divine presence as you spend time in intimacy with the living God. This opens your spirit to believe for something new that is all so much greater than anything that you have ever experienced. In the place of intimate fellowship with God, you enter the realm of 'all things are possible in God'. This replaces the limited vision we have in our natural flesh with a Holy Spirit inspired one that propels us to take steps of faith.

The righteous shall flourish like a palm tree, He shall grow like a cedar in Lebanon. ¹³ Those who are planted in the house of the Lord Shall flourish in the courts of our God. ¹⁴ They shall still bear fruit in old age; They shall be fresh and flourishing, **Psalm 92:12-14.**

The now anointing makes you ever productive and fruitful in your faith to the glory and praise of God. It is ever increasingly productive because it is powered supernaturally above the realm of the natural where things are obstructed by a myriad of reasons. You become a shining spectacle for all to see and offer up praises to God for.

¹⁴ "You are the light of the world. A city that is set on a hill cannot be hidden. ¹⁵ Nor do they light a lamp and put it under a basket, but on a lampstand, and it gives light to all who are in the house. ¹⁶ Let your light so shine before men, that they may see your good works and glorify your Father in heaven. **Matthew 5:14-16**

¹⁶You did not choose Me, but I chose you and appointed you that you should go and bear fruit, and that your fruit should remain, that whatever you ask the Father in My name He may give you. **John 15:16.**

This 'now anointing' propels you to engage in progressive exploits of faith as you advance in the grace of God released upon your life in line with fresh visions you receive through the Holy Spirit. You will leave your mark on the world through exploits of faith in your days here on earth. **Hebrews 11:30-38**

The now anointing makes you a different person, it takes over your life as you yield to His leadership thus enabling you to fulfil divine purpose. King Saul is a case study.

In the early life of Saul, he experienced limited breakthroughs and successes that barely scratched the surface of his ordained purpose in life. Saul was enterprising, took the initiative and was one who had dogged determination to succeed in whatever mission he had at hand, yet he hit a brick wall of limited success in his efforts before the 'now anointing' came upon his life.

There was a man of Benjamin whose name was Kish the son of Abiel, the son of Zeror, the son of Bechorath, the son of Aphiah, a Benjamite, a mighty man of power. ² And he had a choice and handsome son whose name was Saul. There was not a more handsome person than he among the children of Israel. From his shoulders upward he was taller than any of the people. ³ Now the donkeys of Kish, Saul's father, were lost. And Kish said to his son Saul, "Please take one of the servants with you, and arise, go and look for the donkeys." ⁴ So he passed through the mountains of Ephraim and through the land of Shalisha, but they did not find them. Then they passed through the land of Shaalim, and they were not there. Then he passed through the land of the Benjamites, but they did not find them. ⁵ When they had come to the land of Zuph, Saul said to his servant who was with him, "Come, let us return, lest my father cease caring about the donkeys and become worried about us." ⁶ And he said to him, "Look now, there is in this city a man of God, and he is an honourable man; all that he says surely comes to pass. So, let us go there; perhaps he can show us the way that we should go." ⁷ Then Saul said to his servant, "But look, if we go, what shall we bring the man? For the bread in our vessels is all gone, and there is no present to bring to the man of God. What do we have?" ⁸ And the servant answered Saul again and said, "Look, I have here at hand one-fourth of a shekel of silver. I will give that to the man of God, to tell us our way." 1 Samuel 9:1-8.

5

Saul was endowed with innate leadership qualities; he stood tall above all his peers and contemporaries as a very visible leader figure. Saul had tenacity and demonstrated capacity to offer leadership by taking on a very difficult task of scouring the earth to find lost donkeys that belonged to his father even though, this could easily have been done by one of his father's many servants. Sadly, all this very great potential he had was both obscure and limited as a result of him lacking spiritual insight or meaningful encounter with God. In the divine plan to take Saul into a deeper spiritual dimension with himself, God orchestrated that his father's donkeys go missing suddenly. This event provided and opening for Saul's destiny out to come out of obscurity by anointing him with the now anointing that gave him a new vision of the future.

15 Now the Lord had told Samuel in his ear the day before Saul came, saying, 16 "Tomorrow about this time I will send you a man from the land of Benjamin, and you shall anoint him commander over My people Israel, that he may save My people from the hand of the Philistines; for I have looked upon My people, because their cry has come to Me." 17 So when Samuel saw Saul, the Lord said to him, "There he is, the man of whom I spoke to you. This one shall reign over My people." **1 Samuel 9:15-17**

The 'now anointing' ensured that all the prophecies hanging over his head that were yet to be fulfilled in his life were kickstarted into life to ensure their fulfilment. When the 'now anointing 'is lacking, prophecies go unfulfilled. It made Saul abandon the 'small distracting vision of finding the donkeys' give way to the bigger vision of leading the nation of Israel for which God had created him from the foundation of the earth.

19 Samuel answered Saul and said, "I am the seer. Go up before me to the high place, for you shall eat with me today; and tomorrow I will let you go and will tell you all that is in your heart. 20 But as for your donkeys that were lost three days ago, do not be anxious about them, for they have been found. And on whom is all the desire of Israel? Is it not on you and on all your father's house?" 21 And Saul answered and said, "Am I not a Benjamite, of the smallest of

6

*the tribes of Israel, and my family the least of all the families of
the tribe of Benjamin? Why then do you speak like this to me?"* **1
Samuel 9:19-21**

The 'now anointing' ensured that all that were his divinely
apportioned allocation in life was delivered into his hands on a
platter of gold. This portion had been reserved for him but until the
anointing came upon his life, it was not released to him. Similarly,
you need to encounter this now anointing so that you get all that
heaven has allocated for you as you go through life. The anointing
will make people honour and favour you as you go through life. The
'now anointing' takes you from the lowest point in life and qualifies
you to sit with royalty just like Saul experienced.

*[22] Now Samuel took Saul and his servant and brought them into the
hall and had them sit in the place of honour among those who were
invited; there were about thirty persons. [23] And Samuel said to the
cook, "Bring the portion which I gave you, of which I said to you,
'Set it apart.'" [24] So the cook took up the thigh with its upper part
and set it before Saul. And Samuel said, "Here it is, what was kept
back. It was set apart for you. Eat; for until this time it has been kept
for you, since I said I invited the people." So, Saul ate with Samuel
that day. [25] When they had come down from the high place into the
city, Samuel spoke with Saul on the top of the house.* **1 Samuel 9:22-
25**

This now anointing opened the doors to multitude of revelational
encounters with the divine supernatural that totally transformed his
life and path of destiny.

*Then Samuel took a flask of oil and poured it on his head, and kissed
him and said: "Is it not because the Lord has anointed you
commander over His inheritance? [2] When you have departed from
me today, you will find two men by Rachel's tomb in the territory of
Benjamin at Zelzah; and they will say to you, 'The donkeys which
you went to look for have been found. And now your father has
ceased caring about the donkeys and is worrying about you, saying,
"What shall I do about my son?"' [3] Then you shall go on forward*

*from there and come to the terebinth tree of Tabor. There three men going up to God at Bethel will meet you, one carrying three young goats, another carrying three loaves of bread, and another carrying a skin of wine. ⁴ And they will greet you and give you two loaves of bread, which you shall receive from their hands. ⁵ After that you shall come to the hill of God where the Philistine garrison is. And it will happen, when you have come there to the city, that you will meet a group of prophets coming down from the high place with a stringed instrument, a tambourine, a flute, and a harp before them; and they will be prophesying. ⁶ Then the Spirit of the Lord will come upon you, and you willprophesy with them and be turned into another man. ⁷ And let it be, when these signs come to you, that you do as the occasion demands; for God is with you. ⁸ You shall go down before me to Gilgal; and surely, I will come down to you to offer burnt offerings and make sacrifices of peace offerings. Seven days you shall wait, till I come to you and show you what you should do." ⁹ So it was, when he had turned his back to go from Samuel, that God [c]gave him another heart; and all those signs came to pass that day. ¹⁰ When they came there to the hill, there was a group of prophets to meet him; then the Spirit of God came upon him, and he prophesied among them. ¹¹ And it happened, when all who knew him formerly saw that he indeed prophesied among the prophets, that the people said to one another, "What is this that has come upon the son of Kish? Is Saul also among the prophets?" ¹² Then a man from there answered and said, "But who is their father?" Therefore, it became a proverb: "Is Saul also among the prophets?" ¹³ And when he had finished prophesying, he went to the high place.*1 Samuel 10:1-13**

Conclusion

The Benefits of the 'now anointing' could not be sustained in the life of King Saul because of flaws in his character because of his fundamentally unchanged nature despite the anointing upon his life. King Saul, although prophetically selected, correctly anointed by God's representative to his destiny was like old skin trying to contain new wine. After just two years of great exploits, cracks began to show **1 Samuel 11:1-15, 1 Samuel 13:1.** These cracks include those of

Self-will **1 Samuel 13:2.** Pride or compelling desire to take the credit **1 Samuel 13:3-5.** Presumption **1 Samuel 13:7-9.** Fear of the people opinion more than the fear of God's viewpoint **1 Samuel 13:10-12.** Saul departed from following God's commandments by choosing the path of disobedience **1 Samuel 13:13-14**.

Do not be another Saul God would regret anointing because you are unbroken, unchanged, unsaved, and not renewed in your mind by His power, surrender to the Lordship of Jesus over all aspects of your life right here, right now.

ABOUT THE AUTHOR

Stephen Bello is a qualified Agricultural Engineer who has actively taught for close to two decades in secular education across many secondary schools both in Nigeria and the United Kingdom where he achieved QTS status in teaching.

Over the years, he has become an alumnus of the Christ Redeemer Bible College (CRBC) where he lectured for some years. Stephen is a graduate of various schools and courses organised by the Redeemed Christian Church of God Central Office UK such as: 'School of Disciples', Ministers induction course (MIC), Pastors induction Course (PIC). More recently, he became a graduate with distinction of the Advanced Diploma in Ministry (ADM) organised by the National Advisory Board on Education and Training (NABET).

Stephen has a passion for teaching and training, he and his wife serve as lead Pastors in charge of the RCCG Victorious Family Parish in Chatham, Kent. He is an active member of the RCCG Sunday School Ministry, Counselling teams, School of Disciples among others.

Stephen is also active working cross – culturally and inter – denominationally under the banner of Churches Together in Medway (CTIM) where he plays an active role as a champion of ecumenism. He is married to Olabisi, and they are blessed with glorious children.

ACKNOWLEDGEMENT

My gratitude goes first to the Lord who saved me from destruction and drew me unto Himself engaging me in a loving relationship with the triune God through salvation of my soul when He flooded my dark life with His liberating light of truth. I wish to thank the Lord for the multitude of mentors He brought into my life to help form and shape me as I was growing up as a young Christian in the University of Ibadan. I celebrate the leaders and brethren of Christ Apostolic Church Students Association CACSA U. I. branch, they are a true family indeed.

I celebrate the memories of my late parents Mr L.O. and Mrs C.F. Bello who nurtured me and taught me the value of hard work, dedication, commitment, and integrity. I am grateful to my siblings especially Pastor Pius Bello and family for their sacrificial support for me through trying times. In the same vein, I want to thank God for extended family circle of relatives who either through birth or marriage connections stepped into my life at various times. God used many of you to step into the breach in difficult times and you continue to be a source of encouragement to us daily. Thank you so much indeed.

I want to thank God for Pastor Busari of the Assemblies of God Church (AOG) in Jalingo town, Taraba state where I served during my National Youth Service year (NYSC). I am also very grateful to Reverend Lawrence Nwanna of the Resurrection Gospel Mission (RGM) Isolo, Lagos, my first church after completion of my service year from whom I learnt a lot. The Almighty God strategically placed these servants of the Lord in my life to show me the ropes of enduring Christian ministry at my early stages of development.

I am forever grateful for the ministry of the Redeemed Christian Church of God (RCCG) that has impacted my life greatly through the various training, teaching and examples of our coach and role model; Pastor E. A. Adeboye and his ever-supportive wife and true mother, Pastor Mrs Folu Adeboye. I particularly want to thank Pastor Samuel Abiola and his wife for firsthand and first-class training in diligence, commitment, integrity, genuine Christian love, and humility in ministry. I pray that the Almighty God will continue to raise children for you all over the world.

I celebrate my Spiritual Parents in the Lord Pastor 'Leke' & Pastor (Mrs) Bola Leke Sanusi who remain exceptionally great role models in ministry and a catalyst used by God to propel me into the purpose of God for my life and destiny. May the Lord continue to uphold and enlarge your coasts daily all over the world Amen. Your sun shall never go, may you keep on rising higher and higher in Christ daily Amen. **2 Corinthians 3:18**

I am eternally grateful for the ministry involvement, investment in mentoring, prayers, encouragement, corrections, and challenges both directly and remotely of my esteemed Spiritual icons too numerous to mention here. These include the erudite teacher and speakers – Pastor Brown Oyitso and his wife Pastor Helen Oyitso of the RCCG Central Mission Board, great mentoring missionaries to foreign missions. I greatly celebrate Reverend Moses Aransiola and his wife Reverend Mrs Funmi Aransiola of Gethsemane Prayer Ministries International. Their ministry continues to make global impact, I cherish you greatly. I similarly thank the Lord for divinely connecting me through our Spiritual Parents to a whole host of caring Spiritual developers too numerous to mention here who stop at nothing to ensure I become the all-round best always.

I want to thank the Lord for all the leaders of the RCCG in the UK at various levels for facilitating my Spiritual growth in Ministry. I am greatly indebted to the leadership of the RCCG mission in the UK for giving me opportunities to be of service in various teams. I thank all members of RCCG Victorious Family Parish, Chatham in Kent for giving me the privilege to be God's servant to you and for standing by me through thick and thin in often challenging and discouraging circumstances. The Lord will always bless and reward the work of your hands Amen. To my number one fan and supporter 'Bisi' and the girls, I salute your courage and resilience in putting up with me, God bless you.

Stephen Bello, Kent United Kingdom
November 16th, 2023

ABOUT THE BOOK

Aaccording to the bible in the book of Ecclesiastes chapter 3, there is a time and a season for everything upon the Earth including you and your divinely ordained purpose or destiny. When the Lord wants to help an individual, a word aptly spoken is sent to deliver such from destruction.

Hosea 4:6a My people perish for lack of knowledge (vision) …..

This material in your hand is inspired by God to highlight the importance of obtaining and pursuing a God inspired vision for your life. Your dogged commitment to a vision through thick and thin will lead you to the shores of ever constant and evergreen achievements through all your life with the help of God. This material that has been released into your hand would launch you into an unending season of constant comprehensive progressive success as you apply the principles taught therein. Vision will give birth to new levels of success, innovation, enterprise as well as breaking through all obstacles on your way.

I am confident in God that this would propel you into a new season and sustain you on the ladder of progress. It is designed to be a catalyst that will infuse fresh passion to act on divine principles expounded here by His Spirit to whom all credit should go. It is no substitute for diligent hard work, intense prayer, study, meditation or following specific leading of His Spirit but rather a useful companion as you continue your journey to global generational significance through Christ.

May this work propel you on eagle wings forward in every aspect of your life and existence daily Amen. Congratulations on your first step which is laying hold of this material. Once you have caught the fire of Vision, pass it on to others in your sphere as a destiny helper. The world awaits your manifestations.

*Then the Lord answered me and said: "Write the vision and make it plain on tablets, that he may run who reads it.***Habakkuk 2:2**

OTHER BOOKS BY STEPHEN BELLO

https://www.amazon.co.uk/dp/B09DJFB2YT - **My Turn Will Come (eBook & Paperback)**
https://www.amazon.co.uk/dp/B099P2FYV7 - **Divine Success (eBook & Paperback)**
https://www.amazon.co.uk/Learn-Me-Stephen-Bello/dp/B0BRZ4JDQX -**Learn of me (eBook & Paperback)**
For more copies of this and other books by the author Stephen Bello visit www.amazon.com.
Find out more about the works and activities of the author by visiting author.amazon.com.
Kindly send the author your review to the book by e-mail to stephen2bello@yahoo.co.uk or by 01634920491

PONDER ON THIS

If you are willing and obedient, you shall eat the good of the land but if you refuse and rebel, you shall perish Isaiah 1:19-20

AFTERWORD

The journey of a thousand miles starts with the first step. I have no doubt in me that God created you to accomplish great things on earth and to make a positive contribution to society.

Life does not always deal the best cards to us and this in itself could place you at a disadvantage or indeed damage your future chances in life. God the loving creator of all people would like to come alongside you to help you through the ups and downs you might face. His invitation to you is valid today as it has ever been.

28 Come to Me, all you who labour and are heavy laden, and I will give you rest. 29 Take My yoke upon you and learn from Me, for I am gentle and lowly in heart, and you will find rest for your souls. 30 For My yoke is easy and My burden is light." **Matthew 11:28-30.**

Would you respond and come to Jesus today? Would you allow Jesus to help and guide you into the very best that God has for your life? You can do this by inviting Jesus into your heart as your own personal Lord and Saviour.

When you do this from a very sincere heart, all your records of sins before God will get cleaned out, you will become free from the guilt and judgement you rightly deserve because of the sins of your past that God has now forgiven. A new chapter will be open to you to begin to live as the loving God had planned for you all along. Friend, will you consider this and take your first step to reconcile with your maker right now?

Say this player of commitment to God from your heart:

Lord Jesus, I thank you for loving me enough to die for me on the Cross of Calvary to cancel out all my sins.
I come to you today with a heart of true repentance. I am truly sorry for all my sins of the past, forgive me of all of them today.
Give me a new heart that loves you. Come and be my own personal Lord and Saviour from this moment onwards.
Walk with me daily from now on and help e to always please you. Thank you for saving me and making me your child in Jesus name Amen.

If you said that prayer sincerely from your heart, you have now become a member of God's heavenly family here on earth. I want you to share your story using the contact details in the book so we can continue to pray for you.

I want you to also tell your family/friends/colleagues as well as significant people in your life the joy you have experienced. To keep growing in your faith, look for and become a part of a bible believing church where you will be able to grow spiritually.

God bless and keep you day by day in His overwhelming love Amen.

Stephen

EPILOGUE

'For the vision is yet for an appointed time, but at the end it shall speak, and not lie: though it tarry, wait for it; because it wil surely come, it will not tarry.'

Habakkuk 2:3

Printed in Great Britain
by Amazon

32405142R00056